YOU GET TO WIPE A
POOPY BUTT

Memorably Messy Tales for Dads

By Chris Horton

Copyright © 2017 Vacationing Life, LLC.

ISBN-13: 978-0997934823
ISBN-10: 0997934824

DISCLAIMER: The purpose of this book is to share the journey of one dad and his family. It is by no means providing parenting or medical advice. This book shares a glimpse into the life of one dad and the perspective he would like to share with other dads and guys who are ready to become a dad.

Cover Design: Tamsen Horton
Editing: Parenting is not edited.
Layout: Penoaks Publishing, http://penoaks.com

About the author: www.wipeapoopybutt.com
Authors' photo courtesy of Tamsen & Chris Horton

DEDICATIONS

Thanks dad, for all you have ever done. You've always been the example of how to be a good guy in life and an amazing dad for your family.

Love you always.

Kipper and Tadders, thank you for making my daddy adventure one that I look forward to everyday.

You are loved beyond words.

Tamsen, thank you for choosing me to be a part of your life. I love our life, our family and our future.

Your boys love you to the moon and back.

TABLE OF CONTENTS

Who is this book for? 1
Who Am I to Write This Book? 3
Holy Crap! You Are Going to be a Dad! 4
Enjoy the Ride 11
Selling Your House While Pregnant…Is Stupid… 14
First Diaper 21
Dream House? 24
Is Common Sense Really Common? 28
Your Baby is Puking on You. What Do You Do? 31
Get Rid of Your Pregnancy Weight…DAD 34
Power Hour of Awesome Home Cleanliness 37
What Type of Poop Lies Within? 40
Backup Plans 43
Do not drink your wife's wine, when she hates your beer. 47
When in Doubt, Off to the Doctor You Go 48
Loss Sucks 50
Grandparents 58
Kipper Quotes: Kids Say Awesome Things 60
Car Seat Confessions 62
Just Because… 68
The Wipe Scale 73
How Do You Play With a Baby? 76
Bottles Vs. Food Food 80
Live Like Bo 84
Helicopter Vs. Common Sense…The Great Debate 90

Trick or Treat Tootles McGoo... 93

PB&J = Butt Loads of $? 96

You Love _____, Will They? 101

Sleep? 105

Damn You, Fruit Snacks 108

Scrub a Dub Dub, a Shower or the Tub? 112

Token Economy 115

Be the Tickle Monster 118

Some Assembly Required 120

Travel Time with the Spud 122

Little Helpers 125

Sweet Diaper Bag Dude! 127

What? No Hockey?! 130

The Store 132

Get Out and About 135

Car Vs. Minivan Vs. SUV 139

Daycare Dilemma 142

Eyebrow Rubber 146

Be a Dad 148

Splish Splash 152

Going to the Arena 156

Get Into Their World 158

Know the Cry 161

Holy Phantom River of Poop 163

What to Buy? 166

Enter the Minivan 169

What the Hell is Intussusception? 172

Live a Vacationing Life 175

Cover That Tush 177

To Disney or Not to Disney 180

Be a Pirate 185
Sport It Up 188
Diaper Wash 190
The Untimely Poop 192
What? No Bottles? 195
Tag = Worst Dad EVER 198
Pictures, Pictures, and More Pictures 202
Take a Day Off 205
Show Your Kids Where You Work 207
Don't Forget to Say, "I Love You." 210
Now What? 211

Acknowledgements 213
About the Author 214
Thank You 215

WHO IS THIS BOOK FOR?

It's for you.

It's for any guy out there who thinks they want to become a dad.

It's for any guy out there that got the amazing news he is going to be a dad.

It's for any guy out there who is in the midst of trying to get his wife pregnant (not while reading the book), but you get the idea.

It's for the moms out there who want a sneak peak at what a dad is thinking.

It's for my two boys when they are at that special time in their life.

This book is about being a dad.

Every guy has dreams of one day being a dad.

What does that look like for you?

What do you see when you see yourself as a dad?

What are your hopes?

What are your dreams?

What are your fears?

I wrote this book, not to provide advice as much as to lend some perspective of what lies ahead. This is totally based on my perspective and my experiences.

Your adventure will be yours.

Each section of this book provides a little different take on just a fraction of the experiences that await you in the land of being a daddy.

Come on in, pull up a chair or read this while rocking a teething baby.

You are one lucky fella.

Why?

Because…

You get to wipe a poopy butt…

WHO AM I TO WRITE THIS BOOK?

I'm a dad who loves my little boys more than anything.

If you are a dad as well, I'm probably a lot like you. I have a day job, an amazing wife and two great little boys. I don't have everything figured out but I love being a dad and am willing to embrace each day for the wonder and unknown.

If you are not a dad yet, then you should listen to every word I say. Kidding.

I love talking about my boys and my adventures as a dad. This book is a glimpse into our adventures.

I encourage you, as a dad and as a person, to want more. More time, passion and money to live the life you want with your family.

You are worth it. Your family is worth it.

Enjoy.

HOLY CRAP! YOU ARE GOING TO BE A DAD!

What did you feel when you found out you were going to be a dad?

Extreme joy? Fear? Anxiety? Was it your dream come true? Perhaps it was a combo platter of all of the above thoughts and emotions?

No matter what you felt or what you feel right now, *welcome.*

Just as no two kids are the same, no two pregnancies will be exactly the same either. From the moment you find out you are going to be a dad, the journey begins.

I remember when my wife let me know she was pregnant. The flood of emotions that followed was almost indescribable. From that point on, I just felt different. Suddenly, everything was seen with different eyes. You spend so much time preparing for the big arrival day and when it's time to welcome your son or daughter into the world, it's just crazy amazing.

My oldest son Kip was born after forty-seven hours or labor. Have you ever felt like a day lasted forever? Well, those forty-seven hours seemed to go by at a snail's pace.

Being a high-risk pregnancy, my wife was under close monitoring. Our baby's heart rate would go up, and then it would go down. The doctor would come visit and let us know they may take him out in the next couple hours and then come back an hour later to let us know they were going to wait a while. Again, the emotional endurance was something I don't think you could prepare for until you experience it. These are shoes I'm not sure you can understand until you walk a few steps in them. Imagine sitting there in the hospital, watching your wife in pain for almost two days straight. The nurses are telling you the medicine should be helping with the pain, but you see your wife and know it's not touching what she's feeling. You see her heart rate increase and decrease on the monitor as the contractions come and go. Aside from watching your wife in pain, the other emotional rope pulling at you is your baby. Is he ok? The doctors seem concerned and indecisive as to when to bring him out into the world. I finally asked if there was a possibility of just doing a C-section and moving on. Our doctor at the time was very much trying to make our pregnancy end with traditional delivery. She pretty much dismissed the idea of a C-section. What did I know, I was just the guy sitting there watching his wife in pain and wondering about my baby's fluctuating heart rate. I'm not a doctor, but I sure learned a lot about them.

After almost two days, the doctor came for a visit. Tamsen was toast, beyond done, and exhausted. We sat there and listened to our doctor explain to us that our son would not be able to be delivered in a traditional delivery because he wouldn't fit through the birth canal. Come again? Excuse me? We have had all sorts of ultra sounds, exams, poking and prodding and we are *just* finding out that a baby cannot make the delivery journey via the route we have been trying to pursue? So, the C-section was scheduled after being induced for forty-seven hours and a labor that apparently was not going to lead to where we were trying to go. Yup, there's that roller coaster of emotion, looping around and around.

Entering the operating room with my wife on the cold metal table was surreal. All the people, the bright lights, tools in a variety shapes and materials were all there to bring the pregnancy journey to it's conclusion. It's difficult to take the moment in with all the adrenaline rushing through your body, but it's one of those times in your life you will never forget.

Once the procedure began, I had no idea what to expect. My whole world was in this room. I wanted Tamsen to be free of pain and I wanted my baby boy to be safe and out of harms way. Sitting next to Tamsen, I gently rubbed my pointer finger between her eyebrows in a circular motion. I found this to be helpful on stressful nights while she was enduring the adventures of law school. This made law school look like a day at Disney.

The anesthesiologist told me she should only feel a bit of pressure. Ever heard that in a medical setting? A little pressure you say? I can personally recall times where a "little pressure" felt like my soul was being ripped off my bones, but I had to trust them. We were approaching the finish line of this amazing journey.

Kip's head of hair was the first thing I saw, then his face. All while my son is being delivered, I felt like I was there, but I wasn't there. Surreal for sure, where you feel like you are watching a movie or someone else's story. In a matter of a couple minutes, Kip was out in the world. I had never seen a newborn baby in my life. Those Hallmark type movies are full of crap I tell ya! My first reaction was one of horror. Kip was purple and wasn't making a noise. I knew you wanted to hear a baby cry soon after they were born. We didn't hear any crying. They cleaned him off a bit, brought him over the scale to examine, weigh and measure him. He still had not cried or made any sounds. The cord was cut and clamped and I was right next to my new little man. I asked the nurse if I could touch him, she smiled and said, "of course you can, dad." Holy crap, she just called me a "dad". I put my finger by Kip's little hand and said, "hello" for the first time. In a moment I will never forget, baby Kip grabbed my finger and looked right at me. This new little amazing soul was beautiful. I had loved before, but nothing like this. I knew my emotions were unlike anything I had ever experienced or felt before. This was my son, my little boy.

The nurses wrapped Kip up in a generic hospital blanket and brought him over to see an exhausted mama. We smiled, we cried and we were a mama and a daddy.

Moments later, Kip got his first bath and we heard him cry for the first time. He sounded like a little goat.

How can you possibly prepare for this level of emotion?

The BEST possible way to make sure your delivery day and time in the hospital is as ideal as possible is to know you trust your team. You and your wife are embarking on an incredible journey. Who do you want as your tour guide? We learned a very valuable lesson with our first pregnancy. It is essential to know, like and trust your doctors. With Kip, we tried to make the best decision based on what we knew. Many times that's all you can do. But, if something doesn't feel right or you don't like something about your doctor, change it up. You are going to go through every emotion imaginable when on the pregnancy journey. You want a doctor who is more than a doctor. They need to be a real person who can read your situation and treat it accordingly. With our second pregnancy, we chose a different hospital and a different doctor. A close family friend recommended the doctor we went with. Recommendations will come in waves when you are expecting. When you truly know, like and trust who the recommendations are coming from, those are the ones you roll with. Dr. Anita Vandenberg is amazing. She was more than a doctor for us. Anita was like family, helping us grow our family. She's a rare gem in the medical field who guided us through our second pregnancy with our son, Tad. To all the Dr. Vandenbergs out there, thank you. You are what the baby-making world needs more of.

Welcome to the most amazing journey you will ever take. No two days will be exactly the same. Amazing moments will be happening all the time. Smiles that will make your heart feel a way it's never felt before. Milestones will seem to be magical just because they simply happened. You'll witness faces and reactions that are priceless because this is your little boy or little girl. You'll also have poop and pee whirling at you in the middle of the night, typically hitting you with amazing accuracy. It's all awesome and each day is special.

Take the good and the bad.

Take the happy and the sad.

Take the long nights and the gloriously long days.

Enjoy the laughter.

Learn the cries.

Cherish each and every day.

Once again, welcome to the land of being a daddy.

It's freaking awesome.

Your man card just got upgraded.

ENJOY THE RIDE

Being a dad is the most important job you will ever have.

You've got this.

Get strapped in, put your arms in the air and live it. Drink it in.

There are always moments that go by faster than we would like. As Kip was growing up, he would begin to find his own way of saying things. For instance, "ha ha" meant one thing and that one thing was hockey. Kip knew daddy liked hockey and when he was very young, he would see hockey on television and say he wanted to play, "ha ha".

For father's day, when Kip was around two years old, my wife took us to the hockey store. Her plan was to surprise me by getting Kip his first pair of ice hockey skates. It was awesome. There we were in the hockey store, looking at skates the size of my fist. Kip was all about it, because it related to, "ha ha". We picked some out that he thought looked cool and off we went.

When we got home, Kip wanted to wear his skates in the house. That works fine with ice hockey skates and some say it's a great way to break them in, walking on the carpet around the house. I happened to get out my iPad and shoot a video of Kip stumbling around the house in his skates, saying he wanted to play, "ha ha". I love that video. His voice, his movements and the way our house looked at the time, they are all in the past now.

Over time, phrases like, "ha ha" will come and go. That's where enjoying the ride really comes into play. Every kid will have their own phrases, habits and tendencies that makes them uniquely them. Write those moments down as they happen. Take a video or start a journal to enjoy when that time has moved on.

This book is filled with my memories and my experiences that I wanted to share with you and other dads, no matter where they are in their adventure. Enjoying the ride can be a challenge at times, especially when you are in the middle of it. You might be tired, a bit stressed and even unsure at times. Just remember, time will keep moving and enjoying your time as a dad and each phase and age is up to you. You are in control of how you choose to spend each day as a dad. Make it count.

As I said earlier, get strapped in dad. This job is one where you need to expect the unexpected and where you are in complete control of how you approach each day.

Make each day simply amazing.

Being a dad is awesome.

We live, we learn, we grow and try to do better every day.

This book was written for you because I wish I knew more at the beginning of my adventure.

I hope it provides you with a few "heads up" moments that lead to thoughts that will serve you well.

It's your journey, your adventure.

You are in control.

…Even when pee is streaming at you with extreme accuracy…in the dark…

SELLING YOUR HOUSE WHILE PREGNANT...IS STUPID...

Forty-seven hours of labor, multiple offers on a home, a C-section, and then bringing your baby boy home to a house you sold while he was being born. Sound like something you want to sign up for?

We did, it was stupid and here's the story...

When Tamsen and I first got married, we lived in a condo that I bought when I first began teaching. It was my bachelor pad, but not your typical one. It was brand new when I bought it and I kept it up pretty well.

When we found out we were expecting, I had this silly thought in my head that we needed to move. For whatever reason, I did not think it was cool for a kid to live in a condo. Hindsight being what it is, I think it would have been great.

So, Tamsen and I went to a couple open houses one weekend. We came across a house that we really liked. The realtor was nice enough and talked to us about what we were looking for. We really wanted to be on the water. He happened to have a house similar to the one we were visiting and the lot was on the water. He gave us the address as well as the code to get into the key box and off we went.

It was pretty much love at first sight with this house. You have to remember, we were coming from a condo and were looking at a brand new house on the water.

We were in love.

We made the decision at that time that we were going to list the condo and rent an apartment for a year or so to save for this type of house for our family. It sounded so dreamy.

All of this excitement and Tamsen was only a couple weeks away from her due date. Kip was on his way and we were about to complicate the hell out of his arrival.

Common sense apparently decided to take a vacation from our brains at this point in our lives. I painted each room in the condo, we added some nice tile backsplash and listed the condo for a price that was hard to beat. Silly kids. Holy hell had we reached a new level of pregnancy brain.

We had all sorts of action on the condo right out of the gate. The place looked great, it was in a nice area and the price was fantastic. We knew it would sell quickly. We just didn't know or expect what happened next.

Our day had come for Tamsen's induced labor to begin. We made our way to the hospital and set up shop in our room. Tamsen proceeded to endure 47 hours of labor (holy balls!) and eventually the doctor decided a C-section was the best way to get Kip out of mama's tummy.

At the tail end of the labor, Tamsen was exhausted. She had been emotionally and physically drained. Of course, the realtor is going to call right now, right? Well, she did. We had multiple offers on the condo while we were in the hospital and in no way shape or form did either of us want to deal with it.

But we had to.

I listened to the offers and the scenarios surrounding each buyer. Keep in mind Tamsen is in labor while all this insanity is taking place.

Again, 47 hours of labor! Holy balls part 2!

Eventually, I was able to talk to her about it and we decided on an offer and accepted it. Yes, we were still in the hospital. Our unborn son was essentially about to be born homeless.

After Kip was born, we got home on a Tuesday and we closed that night on selling our condo.

We had an apartment lined up for us to rent so we could save money for our dream house. It wasn't ideal, but it also wasn't forever. I wasn't thrilled with it, but it allowed us the chance to save some money for us to build with our dream builders.

Then it happened…

We were quietly relaxing on one of our final remaining nights in our condo when I found it.

(Enter the back-story)

Tamsen and I are always scoping out neighborhoods around the area we live. We love the area. It really has everything we need and places we like to have around us. Good schools, stores, shops, access to the downtown area, a Starbucks and most important, close to grandma and grandpa. One fateful day, we were combing neighborhoods and we saw a beautiful house. It looked like it belonged on Mackinac Island along the lakeshore. A yellow cottage masterpiece of a house was just calling to us. It had amazing curb appeal. It was awesome. Once we saw this house, we said at that time if it ever went up for sale, we would try to get it.

(Exit the back-story)

The yellow cottage masterpiece Mackinac Island looking house was for sale. There it was, staring back at me on my screen. Full color photos of each room teased us. We had to see it. It was on a real estate website and it was just added. The price was reasonable.

I showed Tamsen and we had a moment.

What do we do?

We need to see this house.

What if we like it?

What about the apartment?

What about saving for the dream house?

Balls...

So, I emailed our realtor, attached the listing for the yellow house and told her we needed to see it the next day. It was a Monday and we were supposed to sign for the apartment on Friday that week. How awesome is that? Our realtor got us a showing the very next day. My dad met us at the house, he was super excited about the possibility of us getting this house, I could tell.

We walked in and immediately fell in love with just about everything. It was awesome. You might as well played dramatic music when the doors opened as though a Greek god just entered the room. Tin ceiling in the kitchen, a 30-foot screened in porch in the back, custom crown molding and an open concept that let your imagination wander.

Long story short, we loved the house, put in an offer and accepted the counter offer later that night. Done and done.

What did we just do?

In only a couple weeks time we sold our house, had a baby and bought a house.

Stupid is all I can say. We didn't see it at the time, but it totally drained us. We were toast.

In hindsight, we should have stayed in the condo. But, we had no idea the changes that came along with adding a baby to our family dynamic. On top of that, we had less of an idea of what moving would do to us.

Moral of the story is there will be plenty of unexpected when you are expecting a baby. There is no reason to add an American Ninja Warrior obstacle course to the already rocky waters.

Keep things simple.

Lesson to be learned: Even though a yellow house might be cool and you don't think you should be in a condo with a baby, stay in the condo.

FIRST DIAPER

Standing over the hospital bassinet, looking at my precious newborn son, and suddenly a foreign object is placed in my hand – a diaper. Now mind you, this will be my first diaper change ever. I'm thirty-four years old and under the watchful eyes of my wife and the latest nurse assigned to our care. I'm playing it cool trying to figure out the front from the back of the diaper.

What are the tabby things? Why are there cute characters on something designed to hold pee and poop? I later discovered the cute factor is one hundred percent handled by marketing departments designed to drain all funds from new parents checking accounts.

Back to the moment at hand – it's game seven of the Stanley Cup Playoffs and I feel the pressure to make the winning play. I was worried about messing this up. Kip is in and out of consciousness as I undid the tabby things, finding them very easy to undo, I pulled the diaper off – no poop – whew!

I wasn't ready to face the poop monster. I needed some practice – at least five or so before bringing on the deuce.

I'm fumbling with the new diaper and chatting away with Kip, thinking that we're having this really cool father-son moment and out of the blue, it happened. Pee is streaming into my nostrils. First the left, then the right, I was being assaulted with pee, straight up the nose. GREAT father-son moment!

I'm flailing around like a fish out of water. Tamsen is calmly telling me to cover his business with the diaper I have in my hands, I can't even do that at this point. I'm covered in pee, Kip is covered in pee, the bassinet is covered in pee, so much for pee being the lesser of the two diaper evils. How could this little person possibly contain this much pee…that I am now covered in.

Welcome to the land of being a daddy.

How can you be prepared for the diaper change? First of all, you will want to practice. Familiarize yourself with diapers and practice on a stuffed animal, or better yet, a friend's baby! Practice doesn't always make perfect, but it gets your feet wet with experience instead of pee.

Next, make sure you are prepared. We all get sucked in to the baby's room looking cute like we see on the internet or in a magazine, but is the set up practical? Make sure your baby changing area is set up with fresh diapers, wipes as well as emergency towels. You can still have a cute set up; it just needs to functionally work when it's game time.

Now, I am here to tell you changing diapers is awesome. Yeah, I know, it sounds crazy, but it's true. I have no idea how many diapers I have changed, but I have learned a lot since that first showering experience. Changing a diaper is a moment to talk to your baby and bond; at least it was and still is for me. My son, Kip, is now 6 (born in 2011) and our newest edition, Tad, is 18 months (born in 2015). I'm not jumping for joy when it's time to change a diaper, but I know how quickly, this time, will go by. Make it a time you enjoy, we have that choice.

Quite often, I found myself looking into the eyes of this new little person, just talking about my day. One day in particular, I was talking to Tad about a day that was less than stellar. I ended the conversation with, "Can you believe that?" Tad's response was his tongue sticking out, making a tooting noise and drooling all over himself. See – he understood perfectly. Those conversations can turn a day around.

Get pooped on. Get pee shot up your nose. It's a great story and don't forget, cute sells.

Lesson to be learned: Cover that thing up!

DREAM HOUSE?

What exactly is a dream house for a family? More importantly, what is a dream house for *YOUR* family?

What does it look like?

Are there two stories or is it a ranch?

Lots of land or in a neighborhood?

Build new or buy something already on the market?

Is it in the city, country or the burbs?

Near family or away from them?

What are the schools like?

The questions can go on and on and on...

We started a notebook filled with pictures, ideas, and thoughts all around the dream house idea. This notebook began before Kip was born. Since having kids, the ideas continue to flow but have changed quite a bit.

Prior to having kids, we were all about a modern/cottage feeling house. Very clean lines, simple touches, but very homey. We pictured transoms over each doorway, dark hardwood floors, stainless steel appliances and all sorts of awesome wherever you looked.

Now that we have our two boys, our priorities have totally changed. I am very thankful we didn't build a house prior to having both of our boys. The house we are currently in is fine for now. In many ways, it's pretty similar to what we probably would have built prior to having kids. Simple, cottage-like curb appeal, three bedrooms and two bathrooms on a wooded lot.

The house is great. Of course, there are things about it I want to change, but that's the nature of the beast. As my wife's Uncle Mike once told me, "A house is never completely done."

You will always want to change this or finish that.

One of our favorite things to do is going to open houses. We enjoy getting ideas and checking out spaces that are different than ours. Looking at different locations is also fun.

One random open house ended up changing our ideal house plans moving forward. A couple things I would like in our next home include:

- 3-stall garage

- 4-5 bedrooms (one would be an office)
- Finished basement
- Updated or new construction
- Pool or near the beach
- Indoor gym/basketball court

You might look at that list and think it's pretty common until you get to the last item.

I love looking at houses listed online. We all have our hobbies, one of mine happens to be looking for the perfect/ideal home for my family (not sure it exists, but one can try). One fateful night, I was up looking at homes on my iPad when I found it. Scrolling through the pictures, everything looked updated, functional kitchen, big yard and an indoor basketball court. I was floored. Have you ever been almost asleep, then heard, saw or found something that totally woke you up? That was this moment. I quickly emailed the listing to Tamsen and sat there staring at the images on my screen, imagining how amazing this would be for our family and our boys.

A few days later, we went to the open house and knew this was something we would like to have someday.

Just like that, one open house and my entire perspective on houses have changed. Now our list includes the indoor basketball court. It might seem like a luxury for some, but it just makes sense when you have kids.

How about you? Will your current house fit the bill as your family grows?

Do you build or find an amazing deal on something that's pre-existing?

Only you and your wife know the answer.

You cannot really go wrong when you keep the full picture in mind.

It's a dream house. Dream big.

Lesson to be learned: A house is never totally "done".

IS COMMON SENSE REALLY COMMON?

Do you remember learning to cross the street when you were a kid? First, you were probably told to stop. Next, you had to look both ways. Finally, when the coast was clear, it was safe to go. Sound about right?

Does that common sense approach work in your day-to-day life? I am as guilty of this as anyone of falling into the trap of not stopping, certainly not looking, but definitely going. Sometimes, getting back to basics is the best way to go.

In our fast-paced society, everyone wants answers and information now. Sadly, they will sometimes take what they can find the quickest and roll with it.

When it comes to your kids, are you willing to "roll with it"? There are a butt load of books written on just about any and every topic in the area of babies and raising kids. All sorts of people will be willing to let you know the research they did, what they found out and how it is what is best for your kids.

What's the problem with that?

None of the research conducted involved *YOUR* kids. You know your kids best. Human beings have individualized needs, wants, likes, dislikes and so on. How in the world can a study possibly cover all the bases of every person? Simply put, it can't.

This is where you and that fancy ass common sense of yours comes into play. You know your kids best. When something is advertised as "the best" do you just roll with that endorsement or do you question it? It may be the best for some, but is it the best for *YOU*? That's for you to decide.

Some parents will take anyone's word on things. From clothes, toys, food, parenting skills to schools. If you live in an area that has "amazing schools", what does that mean? Their state standardized test scores were great? Ok, cool. What about the social/emotional environment they provide? How about the arts? Do they have programs within their districts that interest your family? Think, think, think and think some more. Just because something is advertised as the best, doesn't always mean it's the best for you and your family.

At the end of the day, you are looking out for those who matter to you most, your kids and your family.

Lesson to be learned: Make choices that make sense to you. Think.

YOU GET TO WIPE A POOPY BUTT

YOUR BABY IS PUKING ON YOU. WHAT DO YOU DO?

Puke. The dreaded puke.

What do you do when...

- Your baby pukes on you.
- Your baby pukes on itself.
- Your baby pukes on a friend.
- Your baby pukes on a stranger.
- Your baby pukes in a restaurant.
- Your baby pukes in the car.
- Your baby pukes in their crib.
- Your baby pukes on itself while you are changing a stage 5 poopy diaper.

It will all happen...

It might sound strange, but puke for me is like poop in many ways.

When it's your own kid's puke, poop, pee, it doesn't bother me as much. Anyone else's kid, that's a different story. I can handle my own kid's messes because they are my kids.

I don't know how to explain it and it works differently for everyone.

Tamsen is different. Poop is poop, puke is puke and it's all gross, no matter where it comes from.

One day, she was rocking Kip when he was a baby. It was one of those precious moments where a mama is rocking her baby boy. She was smiling at him, he was smiling right back and her and then it happened.

"Blahhhhh!!"

Baby Kip puked right in mama's mouth.

She was so freaked out and disgusted, her natural reaction was to spit it right back at him.

He was crying and she was grossed out.

I don't happen to recall that type of scenario in any of the baby books we read as new parents. So, yes, I had to put it in *THIS* baby book.

Although it's not the most glamorous part of being a parent, we will all get pooped on, peed on and yes, puked on. It just kinda goes with the territory.

How can you effectively prepare for the 3 P's of terror?

Burp cloths in every possible spot around your house are a good start. Understanding that the 3 P's of terror can strike anywhere at any time is another best practice for handling their destructive powers.

We all poop.

We all pee.

We all puke.

As a dad, you just have to be all right with those 3 things hitting you in the face. Hopefully they will not all attack at the same time.

It will happen. Sometimes the best preparation is just to know it will happen.

Lesson to be learned: Know that you will be getting puked, pooped and peed upon as a dad. Just remember, when you are older and need a little help with your bodily functions, you can hurl revenge on your children.

GET RID OF YOUR PREGNANCY WEIGHT...DAD

Yup, I said it.

The more I look around, the more dads I see looking as though they are trying to get rid of baby weight. You and I both know the pressure people put on moms to rid themselves of their pregnancy weight. What about dads?

When I see a couple pushing a stroller around, the mom looks like she is on her way to regaining a form she's cool with. Dads on the other hand (not all, but they are out there, oh yes, they are out there), tend to throw in the towel once they become dads.

We live in West Michigan. It's known as "Beer City" U.S.A. We love our beer, our breweries and apparently our bellies. That's not an excuse, but a reality. We have some amazing breweries that continually create amazing new concoctions. The result can be a bunch of flabtastic dads roaming the streets.

Please know, I am pointing the finger at all dads, including myself.

Even though I enjoy pizza, beer, ice cream and all sorts of other belly enhancing, carb loaded enticements; I try to maintain some balance.

On the weekends, I cook up about six pounds of boneless-skinless chicken breasts, brown rice and beans. Once the food is cooked, I get out some Tupperware containers (usually about 12) and make ready-made meals for my upcoming week. I take 2 of these with me to school, along with a couple apples, some veggies, and water. During the five days of the week that I am at work, that's the food I'm trying to make my main intake. Clean and healthy food the majority of the time is my attempt to keep some balance.

Aside from food, I get up early (between 3:30 and 4:00 a.m.) to head to the gym 3-4 times a week. I belong to a 24/7 gym and I have the whole place to myself at that time of the day. It's great. I love lifting weights and I use this time as my, "me time". We all need our, "me time". What's yours?

Aside from the food and gym time, I try to play ice hockey once in a while. It's a passion of mine that just brings me pure joy.

I am not sharing this part of my life to say, "hey look at me and all the cool things I do". I'm sharing it because I know it's hard work to eat right, get time to workout and enjoy a hobby. All of this gets even more difficult when you become a dad.

If I can do this, anyone can. You just need to make up your mind that you are going to schedule the time to allow yourself the chance for some "you time".

Aside from making yourself healthier and feeling better, you also show your little ones a great example of being active and eating the right foods.

Balance is the key.

It's just my take.

Lesson to learn: Keep *YOUR* pregnancy weight in check.

POWER HOUR OF AWESOME HOME CLEANLINESS

Some people think that when you have kids, it's ok to let your house go to hell.

Not this guy.

That being said, it can be tricky to keep your house clean with your busy schedule and the time you want to spend with your family.

How do you find the balance needed to keep your house clean and your sanity intact?

Enter the *POWER HOUR OF AWESOME CLEANLINESS* (dramatic music).

How does it work?

So, this is my wife's creation and we roll with it on the weekend. Saturday morning seems to be our go-to day. We give everyone tasks that they need to try to complete during an hour. My wife, Kip and I all have chores that we know fall in our areas of strength. For instance, Kip can dust the baseboards the best because he is the most mobile member of the team who is also the closest to the ground.

My wife is awesome at organizing, so that's her area. I like to get things clean. Like CLEAN clean, so I get the bathrooms and any area we want super clean. We usually tag team laundry and dishes throughout the week.

We keep up on laundry by doing at least a couple loads a day. That way, we don't get behind. A couple loads of laundry a day in our house seems to make sense. It's a rare deal where we get behind.

The key to success with the power hour of awesome cleanliness is that everyone must chip in and buy into the idea that the main cleaning day is once a week. When everyone is on the same page, it can sort of turn into a game. In fact, make it a game. Put Popsicle sticks out on the counter and a different colored plastic cup for each member of the family who is old enough to help out (Tad is not quite there yet). Whoever gets the most sticks (maybe assign a point value to each stick based on the level of difficulty of each task) wins some sort of prize. Maybe they get to choose the spot for dinner that night or what kind of ice cream you buy at the store for dessert.

No matter what, I can tell you, it feels really good when that hour is done. We put in that hour and call it good when the hour is up. The areas you may have missed become a priority for the next week.

This system works for us.

Find one that works for your family.

Lesson to be learned: Have the plan to keep your house clean. Make it fun.

WHAT TYPE OF POOP LIES WITHIN?

To think all poop is created equal is just plain foolish, maybe even droolish, depending on the type of poop that lies within the diaper at hand.

There are actually stages of poopy diapers. A rating system if you will. The system is determined by a few factors. These factors include the number of wipes you need, consistency of the poop in question and the amount. All of these factors can come at you with a different level of intensity.

Hence the stages...

Stage 1: False alarm, no poop; just some tooting.

Stage 2: Just a schotch of poop, a wee lil bit, one wipe.

Stage 3: A formidable amount of poop, maybe solid with a little liquid; possibly 3-5 wipes.

Stage 4: No solid, mostly liquid with a bit of drool poop mixed in. This is a mess, requiring more than 5 wipes.

Stage 5: Might have to tag team this monster. Poop is everywhere and spreading *fast*! Liquid ooze making you question if you can possibly handle this dripping gushing beast. To say this is a mess is an understatement. Your little bundle's hands and feet are suddenly covered in poop and everything within a 2-foot radius has some sort of poop evidence on it.

Stage 6: Holy balls, just take them to the shower.

No matter what stage you find yourself in. Poop has its way of working into your day one way or another.

In fact, just this morning, I was rocking Tad around 5 a.m. He was awake and chatting away while sitting on my lap. All of the sudden, he gets a big grin on his face and lets an awesome toot rip. He made me stop and think if that was just a toot or if he was filling his shorts.

Ended up just being a toot (or as Kip calls it, a "tooty ta ta").

Poop will happen.

You poop. I poop. That gorgeous super-model poops.

We all poop.

No matter what, when there is poop involved…

You get to wipe a poopy butt…

You lucky dog…

YOU GET TO WIPE A POOPY BUTT

BACKUP PLANS

Always have backups.

I don't care if it's diapers, clothes, food, or toys. Everywhere and anywhere you should always have backups. Become Bond-like in your ability to have what you need whenever and where ever you need it.

As a dad, you should almost become paranoid that you don't have enough of something, somewhere.

For instance, my biggie is diapers. I want to make sure I have the right size and the right amount in several strategically thought out places. The car, the van, the diaper bag, the beach bag, the changing table, grandma's and grandpa's, everywhere and anywhere. Don't forget the wipes!

Right after diapers are back up clothes for the baby. If you have a stage 5 blowout and you are away from home, you will not only need a butt load of wipes, but also you will more than likely need new clothes for your little spud. There is a reason packages of wipes are so large, you need about 1,000 at a time; just something to keep in mind. Poop loves to watch you squirm. A baby's hands tend to wander anywhere and everywhere when a diaper change is taking place. Poop covered junk can lead to poop covered hands, legs and before you know it, it's everywhere. Shower time!

Food would be next on my list of back-ups. As Tad has grown, he wants to eat more people food. He still loves a good bottle, but he enjoys crackers, applesauce, baby food and pretty much anything he can gnaw on (while teething). Wherever we go, we pack a cooler. Within the cooler, we bring a couple bottles, ready to go, with backup powder in a container. Aside from that, we bring a pack of graham crackers or saltines and some applesauce packets. You do not want to run out of food. That's just not good for anyone.

Backup plans are not just for things, they are also for intentions.

You might plan on going to the beach, but what if your little ones are asleep when you arrive. One rule we live by is not to awaken a sleeping baby. I know I don't like getting woken up and babies need their rest. So, if your original plan included playing at the beach and you arrive there, only to find sleeping kiddos, what do you do? I keep my tush in the driver's seat and we drive around, looking at beach houses. We drive around until the kids wake up. We live about 40 minutes from Lake Michigan, so it's not a really big deal if our boys fall asleep. We always have a backup plan.

How about when life happens?

One day after school, I get a call from my mom letting me know she had to take my dad to the hospital because he was having chest pains. They had been there all day. I called Tamsen to let her know I was going to the hospital. Times like this are when you need to have your "go to" backup plans as a parent. Tamsen is home with our boys all day and she's ready to "tag out" for a while when I get home. Obviously, we were both concerned about my dad, but we also have two little guys to think about. We need to keep our cool around them; this is their grandpa after all. Also, Tamsen needed to have an alternate plan in place since I wasn't going to be home. She's great at this. The time of the year is a huge factor in Michigan. Fall, spring or summers are easiest, we have a ton of parks and as I said, the beach is a short drive away. The winter can be a bit trickier. You want to make sure that you and your wife both have backup plans for when life happens because we all know it will.

What about when party plans poop on your parade?

For Kip's fifth birthday, we had planned a pool party at a club we went to near our home. We invited all his friends, had the food planned, the custom cake made and all set for this one day. It ended up thunder storming on that day. Poop parade indeed. What do you do? With the magic of social media, my wife informed all the guests that we would be having a party at our house instead. After all, we already had the cake, balloons, and party favors. We made a mad dash to the store, got some party food as well as beer and wine for any of the parents who were awesome enough to roll with our changes. The kids had a great time and Kip had a great birthday party. Even the best-intended, most well planned out events can get rained out. Backup plans once again show their importance.

Expect the unexpected. Have a plan A, B, C and maybe even a plan D.

Remember, you are in charge of the ship. Chart a course with many options that all lead to the same place.

Lesson to be learned: Always have backup plans. Life has a way of showing you where you are missing a backup plan.

DO NOT DRINK YOUR WIFE'S WINE, WHEN SHE HATES YOUR BEER.

Yeah, I did that once. It wasn't the best idea.

Stay away from your wife's wine.

WHEN IN DOUBT, OFF TO THE DOCTOR YOU GO

Do I need to say anything else?

When you are not sure what's going on when your little person is not feeling well, off to the doctor you go.

We are very lucky to live in an area that has an amazing children's hospital, probably one of the best in the country. If we think something is up with one of our boys, we skip urgent care and go right to the hospital. My faith in urgent care has dwindled down to nothing ever since they diagnosed severe heartburn as a heart attack in yours truly. I know the people have a job to do and they do it to the best of their ability, I just don't screw around when it comes to my boys. I want to know I'm not wasting my time and that my boys are getting the best care possible.

Case in point. One day, I was at work and the day came to an end. We had an event that night at the school where I teach. The ladies I work with and I went out for dinner. After dinner, my wife called to let me know Tad, our little guy (5 months old at the time) was having these little episodes where he would begin to shake. We weren't sure if they were seizures or what was going on. I could tell my wife was nervous about it (she's a lawyer and was pre-med, it takes quite a bit for her to get nervous) and I didn't skip a beat. "Get to the children's hospital". When in doubt, you get to the children's hospital; don't screw around. I let the ladies I work with know and they understood that family comes first. Off to the children's hospital, I went to meet up with Tamsen and my boys. We spent forever there, after blood work, tests and waiting for the symptoms to come back. The doctors concluded that it was an "infant tremor" that can happen when a baby gets excited. It made sense and after a long night, leaving around midnight, we were ready to go home. The infant tremors can apparently come and go. We haven't seen them again since that night in June of 2016.

No matter what you know or don't know, when in doubt, get to the children's hospital with your baby and/or kids. I have no problem making these visits because I want to make sure my guys are all right.

If you know what's going on, cool. If you are not sure, be dad enough to admit you don't know what's up and you need to head to the children's hospital.

Better safe, period.

Lesson to be learned: Read the line above.

LOSS SUCKS

We were heading to our baby doctor visit; it was late in the afternoon. Tamsen and I were so excited because today was the day. This is the visit where we get to hear the baby's heart beat. What an exciting time! As we approached the building, I just remember feeling good, excited and proud of the fact that we were on the road to becoming parents.

As we waited in the waiting room, I noticed pictures of babies and kids everywhere. On the magazines, on the walls, in infant carriers in the waiting room, making baby noises. I was just looking forward to the day when I would get to see and meet my new addition to our family.

The nurse enters the waiting room, "Tamsen?" "Oh, here we go." Tamsen and I both smiled with joy and excitement as we headed back to the room where our appointment was to take place. The nurse came in almost immediately and began some small talk, took Tamsen's blood pressure, all the usual. From there, she asked if we wanted to try to hear the heartbeat. Of course, we did! She got out her heart beat monitor tool thing (technical term), put the gel on it and began to move it around Tamsen's tummy. She continued to move it around and kept trying to find where the baby was. The nurse went on to say that at this stage, the baby could be hiding because they are so small at this time of the pregnancy. Eventually, she stopped looking and left the room.

I had a nervous, sick feeling in my guts at that point. What the hell was going on?

You know when you can just read a situation? When your "gut" instinct is talking to you? My "gut" was telling me things I didn't want to think.

The doctor came in. Now, mind you, this doctor had all kinds of credentials. He was quite creepy, though, just in general, I don't know what it was about him. He was just an older guy who wanted to share how smart he was about everything. Also, he was quite a chauvinist, you could hear it in the way he muttered every word. To follow that up, he had the personality of a tic-tac. You may be picking up on the fact that I didn't like him much. You win the prize.

He gets out the monitor, gives it a go, nothing. From there, he checks Tamsen and when he is done he goes on to tell us there is no heart beat. The guy was doing his job, I know that, but the way he told us was something I will never forget. He was so cold and it was almost like the emotional part of his soul had died years ago. Not only did he tell us there was no heartbeat, he went on to tell us that we would have to make an appointment to expel the matter. Are you fucking kidding me?! I was an emotional mess. Disbelief, pain, sadness, anger, depression and all sorts of things I never felt before rushed through my body.

I wanted to expel his Dr. Honeydew ass out the window.

An emotional train wreck...

Tamsen and I left the office completely numb. What just happened? I had just put the crib together the weekend before this appointment, we bought baby clothes, had dreams of the little person we had already begun to love. All of that was crushed in about 15 minutes.

I had never felt this level of "suck" in my life.

Tamsen was supposed to have a class that night (she was still in law school), so I drove her to school and she went in to talk to the professor to let him know she wouldn't be in. I can't imagine how hard that conversation was. While she went into the school, I called my parents. They were SO excited to finally being on the road to becoming grandparents. My mom was crushed. I couldn't tell if she was crushed because of our loss or because her son was in so much pain.

We eventually made it home. We cried. Holy shit, did we cry. We needed to cry. It seemed like we should have run out of tears those next few days.

After that day, it was strange. I would be in a store, hear a song that for some reason made me think about being a dad and that I wasn't going to be anymore. I began to cry in the store. It was messed up.

What the hell was going on?

You went through a crazy emotional trauma. Each of us reacts differently and it's ok.

You don't really get over a loss. It sucks.

Once we had the OK from our *NEW* doctor to begin trying again, we did. After a few weeks, Tamsen gave me the great news that we were pregnant again. I was so excited, so was she. We talked all the time about keeping our hopes in check and everything would be fine this time.

A bit into the pregnancy, I don't recall how long, Tamsen called me at school. "I'm bleeding", she cried to me on the phone. We made an appointment to get in as soon as we could to see if we had another loss. It was about the same time frame as our previous loss.

Sadly, our guard was up and we had lowered our expectations on what is supposed to be a time of great joy.

I remember walking in a downtown area of a little town we enjoy, sipping a coffee and grabbing a seat on a park bench. We just sat there and cried. We were preparing ourselves for our second round of heartbreak.

When we went into the doctor's office, we soon realized that when you have a loss, you get a fast pass of sorts. They seemed to prioritize us to get us in and get us looked at. They went right to the ultrasound, this time, no little heart beat machine. Tamsen lay on the table; I was holding her hand, expecting the bad news.

I was already feeling numb.

That sick feeling in the pit of your stomach.

Then, we heard it.

"Wobble wobble wobble wobble wobble" the sound of a little heart beat.

The ultrasound tech was an angel. We had just met her, but she knew our story and she had a heart of gold. She cried with us and told us our little baby was doing great. Emotional drain in all regards that day. Today, the emotional drain was in another direction.

That ultrasound tech told us to call her if we ever just want to hear the heart beat, she would get us right in. We took her up on the offer many times. We were so lucky to meet this sweet lady. She understood and got it, in every way. Medicine could use more people like our angel ultrasound tech.

Later on in the pregnancy, we had an appointment scheduled before we were to fly to Princeton, New Jersey for Thanksgiving with my wife's family. This appointment was the one where you *COULD* find out if you were having a boy or a girl. Tamsen and I are planners. There are enough surprises with pregnancy and we wanted to know who was in mama's tummy!

My dad came along and the show was on. The tech got the gel out and began to look at our little friend.

"Do you want to know the sex?"

"Yes, we do!"

She smiles, "here you can see the baby's head and there is the spine, everything looks good."

Ok, she must have thought this was funny, teasing us like this.

Penis or vagina was all I wanted to hear.

"There is the heart, beating very well."

Penis or vagina?

"Here are the lungs."

PENIS OR VAGINA! (I wasn't really yelling this at her. Although that would have been pretty damn funny)

"Here are the testicles and the penis"

WOOO HOOO!

Honestly, we didn't care what the sex of the baby was. We just wanted a healthy baby.

We had just met Kip. My precious boy, Kip.

Seeing Kip, ultrasound after ultrasound slowly healed some of the wounds we experienced. He was a kicker. Those legs were always moving and they still haven't stopped.

Losses suck. There is no kind way to put it. They suck. They happen, but they suck. Sadly, we have quite a few friends who have been through multiple losses. It sucks beyond suck because they will be great parents.

It's odd that sometimes you see people with 5 kids and they don't appear to care about them or have the skills needed to raise 1. Yet, they can apparently just shoot kids out on command. On the other hand, you have other people who try and try and try and cannot keep a pregnancy or get pregnant.

No one said this game was fair. If you have had or have a loss, I'm beyond sorry. It's such an emotional roller coaster. It's just awful. My best advice would be to talk to your wife, be open about your feelings, and allow your feelings to happen.

That day when I heard Kipper's heartbeat for the first time made quite a bit of the pain of loss disappear. I can't guarantee that; it was just my experience.

As I sit here today, rethinking about these painful and joyous moments, it makes me realize how lucky we are to be dads.

Take no day for granted.

Each day is precious.

Live it and love those kids.

Lesson to be learned: Live, love, and matter.

GRANDPARENTS

Looking back on my memories with my own grandparents - I was a lucky little boy. Friday night sleepovers with Wheel of Fortune and root beer floats – life didn't get any better than that! These memories are unique between my grandparents and me – Wheel of Fortune and root beer floats weren't happening with mom and dad.

Once we knew Kip was on his way, grandma and grandpa were excited! They had waited thirty-four years for the tea parties, the pirate adventures, trips to the park, and more crafting than Martha Stewart has ever done.

Your parents will have their own take on the role of being a grandma and grandpa. Some people will be super involved; others will be less than ideally involved. My parents are about 10-15 minutes away from our house. It's very normal for Kip to wake up and immediately call grandma and grandpa. He loves them for who they are and it's been so fun to watch their relationship with him grow. They have developed their own unique adventures: the dollar store, playing pirates, decorating with grandma's collectibles – all things that are special between the three of them just like Wheel of Fortune and root beer floats were for me and my grandma.

Each age will be different for you and for your parents. Welcome them always. Let them create their own adventures.

I am beyond lucky with what I have for Kip and Tad. My parents are awesome grandparents.

Lesson to be learned: Grandparents will have their own special way of being grandparents – let them.

KIPPER QUOTES: KIDS SAY AWESOME THINGS

"I play ha ha" (I want to play hockey)

"Don't cheese me" (Don't take my picture)

"Dad, when I pee, it comes out so fast that it shoots back at me!" (When he pushes his pee out so hard, when peeing at a urinal, that it splashes back at him)

"Look at what I made!" (After a large poop)

"Your arm is the best" (When getting cozy during a movie or a nap)

"Dad, I just lifted a pretty big tree branch, now my muscles are like Hulk smashes' (flexing). (He knows I like to lift, always trying to impress me)

"Dad, could you lift our house?" (Of course, I could)

"Here comes the jay bird, here comes the jay bird." (When Kip is running naked around the house after a bath)

"When grandpa and grandma were on their cruise, they were gone so long, I was almost a daddy!" (They were gone 2 weeks)

"Tad is awake, I can sense it." (Jedi wisdom)

"You get to wipe a poopy butt." (When…well, you get the point)

"Why would someone do that?" (After walking past someone with a lot of tattoos)

"Check out my moves" (When performing his dances, ninja moves or being a superhero)

"Woo hoo! My dad and I are destroying a T-Rex" (Playing a dinosaur game at Dave and Busters)

These precious quotes come early and often. Be sure to get a journal to write them down. A great quote from your little one can make you belly laugh like you didn't know you could anymore.

CAR SEAT CONFESSIONS

How many car seats do you plan on buying for your kids?

How many for each?

What features are you looking for in a car seat?

What brand makes the "best"?

Where do you buy it?

Before Kip was born, we asked a friend who had a little one to meet us at the baby store. We "borrowed" her younger daughter to try out car seats and strollers. She was great about it and it helped us see a real life example of how to strap a baby into a seat and how to make a choice that we were comfortable with. I would highly recommend borrowing a friend's kids when testing out these higher priced, very important purchases.

Let's start with the first question.

How many car seats do you plan on buying for your kids? Car seat companies plan out their lines of car seats with the intention of selling you multiple car seats. Take a look...

Infant Carrier- For Kip, we got the Chico Keyfit 30. That seat met our needs and it was great. It's intended for babies 4-30 pounds, comes in cool colors and is reasonably priced. The seat was easy to install and delivered all it said it would.

For Tad, we got the UPPAbaby Mesa infant car seat. This seat was a bit pricier ($100 more), but was crazy easy to install and fell in line with other UPPAbaby products we have purchased in the past. We love this car seat. It's made for babies 4-35 pounds. With Tad being a bigger baby (9 lbs. 11 oz. at birth and 28 pounds at 8 months) it was nice to know we had a little more wiggle room with this seat.

Convertible Car Seats- For Kip, we went with the Britax Advocate. This seat is no longer made but has been updated to the Britax Advocate Clicktight. This seat retails at $439.99, but I found it as low as $352.00 on a website that offers free shipping and free returns. It pays to look around. The convertible seat is made for kids 5-40 pounds rear facing and 20-65 pounds forward facing. Yes, you saw that correctly, you could start your baby in this type of seat if they are over 5 pounds. We will get back to that in a bit.

For Tad, this is where we are. Trying to figure out which seat makes the most sense. There is a boatload of options and we will cover those after I show you the intended plan laid out by car seat manufacturers.

Combination Harness/Booster Seats- Kip currently has one of these in my wife's minivan (got to love the minivan) and one in my car. He has the Britax Frontier Clicktight in the van and the Britax Pinnacle Clicktight in my car. They both do the job, but the Pinnacle is the top dog for this type of seat in my world. It's rather easy to install, has loads of protection (it's a beast) and it has cup holders. Of course, the Pinnacle is the top in the Britax line and retails for $389.99 (I found it online for $312.00). This should be the last seat we have to buy for Kip because it converts into the regular booster seat that can take up to 120 pounds.

Ok, so there are actually more types of car seats than listed, but for this discussion, this will work fine. Do you see the progression from seat to seat? Weight limit and height determine what seat is appropriate for kids. Not age.

Say you go through the progression listed above and you go the route I went.

Infant Seat= $299.00

Convertible Seat= $352.00

Combo Harness/Booster= $312.00

Total= $963.00

*That's getting deals, shopping online, free shipping, all that jazz.

So, you go through and buy each of those seats and you end up around $1,000 by the time you are done.

Let's get back to the convertible seat's weight guidelines. They are listed to start at 5 pounds and go up to 65 pounds. Shouldn't that be the starting point? Can you eliminate the need for the infant carrier? Of course, that all depends on you. You know you best and what you want your experience to be.

Honestly, we bought an infant carrier for Kip because we thought that's what you had to do. We didn't even think twice because the whole baby world was so new and overwhelming. When we decided to have another baby, we had a long discussion about whether to get another infant seat (Kip's had expired). We decided to get one simply because we live in Michigan and Tad was born in December. I didn't want my wife to have to try to get a baby out of the car, slip and have any accidents. The baby carrier made sense based on the time of year Tad was born.

Now, Tad is 18 months old and has moved out of that seat. He is now rolling in his convertible car seat.

Your car seat journey is one that is worth researching.

Ok, so, there are three main types of seats and we know each has a specific job. Cool. What about brands and price points? When it comes to brands, Britax has been a time-tested leader in safety. For me, that's what it's all about, keeping your little spud safe.

There are companies out there that are trying to create an "all in one" car seat. Keep trying. I can't help but recall every other product that promises to do so many things that it ends up failing and falling flat on its face.

When you are looking at car seats, be sure to look at the construction. Is it made of plastic or metal? What sort of impact protection systems does the manufacturer promote? What type of fabric is it made with? Does the seat adjust to ensure maximum protection at multiple heights? Would you trust the seat to protect YOUR baby? That's the biggest question.

You get what you pay for. When it comes to car seats that seems to be an old saying that rings true. No matter what the brand is, take a look at the cheapest, mid price range and the mac daddy top of the line seat. The mac daddy always wins in my book simply because the protection is amazing. That is what I put value in and what I am willing to spend money on.

The car seat adventure can be complex and overwhelming if you let it. Don't. I hope I have provided a bit of guidance that can demystify the experience.

Remember, at the end of the day, your job is to be a dad. Part of that gig is providing protection where and when you can. Strapping that little bundle into a car seat should be something you're in control of. You get to choose the level of protection and in my book; you go all the way to the top.

Lesson to be learned: Go big or go home big daddy!

JUST BECAUSE...

Bring your wife flowers. Bring her the favorite bottle of wine. Take her out to dinner. Bring your kids an unexpected surprise, ice cream, a little toy, something that will make any random day just a little sunnier.

Do you remember that time that one person did that one thing that made you happy? It came totally out of the blue, you weren't expecting it, but it made your day? Someone thought of you. It wasn't your birthday or a holiday. They just thought about you and wanted to do something nice for you.

Have you ever had that happen?

More than likely, we've all had that happen.

It doesn't have to be anything Earth shattering. It's just something where someone else thought about you and did something awesome just because you are you and they love you.

Thinking about any specific examples?

Oh, pick me, pick me...

One day, I was in line at Starbucks. It was a regular day, not even sure what day of the week it was. It was a workday and I was on the way to school. I had about 4 cars in front of me and I was listening to local sports radio. I ordered my mocha venti and continued the waiting game in line. When I eventually made my way to the cashier, they let me know the car in front of me had paid for my coffee.

What?! Why? Who were they? Why did they do that?

They just wanted to do something nice. It was part of that whole, "pay it forward" thing that's out there.

It was awesome. My day took a new direction. I wasn't in a bad mood before getting my coffee that morning, but it sure made me a bit sunnier the rest of the day. Someone intentionally made a choice to make me happy just for the reason of making me happy. They didn't want anything back other than the good vibes they got from knowing they made a stranger's day shinier.

It worked. I was like a beaming ray of flipping sunshine!

Now, what happens?

Now, when I go to Starbucks, I keep my eye on my rearview mirror. If the person behind me seems a bit stressed, I buy their coffee. I want them to feel the way I felt when I got up to the cashier and found out someone wanted to make my day better just for the sake of making my day better.

Have you ever felt anything like that?

If you have, cool. If you haven't, it's time to start putting that kind of awesomeness into the world. Most of the time, you have to put it out there to get it back. Try it sometime. Giving the coffee is just as cool as getting it.

What if we could take this kind of thinking and bring it into our home?

Why wouldn't you?

If we are willing to "make the day" for a total stranger (which is awesome), why wouldn't we do it for the people we care about the most?

We want to inspire, love, acknowledge, comfort and bring joy to those in our family. That's in the job description of being a dad, if there was a job description. There should be. It would be in there. Don't you think?

Have you ever brought your wife flowers on a day (any day) just because? If it's been a while, that might want to be added to the "to-do" list. Now, it shouldn't be something you do because you feel you *HAVE TO*. It should be something you do simply because you know it will make the mother of your children's day brighter. If flowers are not her thing, you know what is. Life as a dad can get busier and busier. We need to take the time to continue to do the little things that make us an awesome husband as well as an amazing dad.

How about your kids? I love surprising Kip. It doesn't have to be anything huge. When I get home from school, he's ready for some dad time. Your kids are ready to see you as well. Some days work better than others, but I try to surprise him once a week with something that I know will make him shine. It can be something as simple as getting home from work and asking him if he would like to go to the park. He loves that time. During the hockey season, I might surprise him with a Wednesday night downtown dinner with dad and game at the arena. You know your kids best. Surprise them. Just because and that's reason enough.

There does not EVER have to be a reason to make someone happy.

Every morning when the students at my school are entering the building at 8:20, I am in the hallway giving high fives, joking around and saying good morning. One day a student asked me why I am in such a good mood. My response, "You're here! This is going to be a great day!"

Shock those you care about with love and surprises that will make them glow.

The world cannot get enough of it.

Lesson to be learned: Whatever makes you happy, do more of it. Whatever makes others happy, provide more of it. Just because…

THE WIPE SCALE

Have you ever stopped to think about why they sell baby wipes in such large packages?

Are they trying to save you money?

OR

Maybe there are so many wipes in a package because you can literally plow through a package of those in a few days when *the poop* is attacking.

Either way, there is a scale to determine how many wipes you will need for each diaper change.

Enter.... *The Wipe Scale* (dramatic music)

The Wipe Scale is based on a non-scientific totally un-researched, yet highly common sense laden set of principles that may serve you well.

1 wipe = courtesy after a wet diaper when mere remnants of poo appear.

2 wipes = courtesy wipe and the follow-up jingle.

3 wipes = there may be poop in this diaper. Depending on the amount of time elapsed between poop leaving the tush and the actual wiping of the poop from said tush, 3 wipes might do the trick.

4 wipes = solid poop. Wipe with care and be sure to check the "nut creases" on the boys. Poop tends to enjoy hiding in these little crevices.

5 wipes = solid poop with the follow-up jingle of some liquid poop. This situation provides a dangerous combo platter and a formidable adversity. 5 wipes should do the trick. Again, in boys, be mindful of the nut creases.

6 wipes = very little solid poop, possibly a combination of drool poop and liquid mess. Nut creases have been invaded and you may need some butt cream once the 6 wipes have cleared the path.

7 wipes = full on liquid poop attack. The nuts of boys are immersed in poop and there is the danger of their hands grabbing their junk. Poop covered hands are never good or socially acceptable. Butt cream is highly recommended upon completion of use of the 7 wipes.

8 wipes and above = when you reach this level, you are in a world of poop. This may require reinforcements and a shower to actually clean off the entire amount of poop within the crevices, creases, and cracks.

If this scale makes sense to you, awesome, common sense and you are friends.

There will be days where there will be no time to determine the number of wipes you will need to tackle the poop beast. On those days, just keep pulling those things out of the package until the poop has been destroyed.

Again, there is a reason they sell wipes in packs that are so large.

You may be thinking, "Who would actually take the time to think about how many wipes they are going to use when wiping a poopy butt?" That's a great question.

I have no idea, but it was fun to write.

Wipe away daddy-o.

HOW DO YOU PLAY WITH A BABY?

You get home from the hospital, begin to unpack your bags, get laundry going, and maybe even make a list of groceries you need to get. Then, it hits you. Ok, we are home now. Now, what?

Now, you live.

What am I supposed to do with my baby?

Well, the baby will more than likely do some basic things at first. They will more than likely spend a great deal of time sleeping, eating, peeing, pooping and looking at you. That's the exterior life of a baby. If you stop to think about it, your baby is going through a ton of "new". Everything is new to them. There are new sounds, sights, touches, tastes, and smells, pretty much everything that it means to be alive. We need to think like a baby at times and attempt to consider things through their minds.

Can you imagine hitting a reset button in your brain and taking everything you currently know and flushing it down the toilet? Starting completely over. What if you were given a completely clean slate? Think about all of the things you wouldn't know.

- Hot and cold
- Light and dark
- Milk and water
- Wet and dry
- Happy and sad
- Comfort and pain
- Why your tummy hurts
- How to communicate your needs
- What you like and don't like
- Why you laugh when someone tickles you
- Why you poop and pee
- Why do I have this? (The junk)

Babies' start with a clean slate and it begins being filled with points of reference the minute they enter your arms. It's our job to keep this mindset in mind when creating experiences for our baby.

One area that I struggled with when Kip was born was playing. I looked forward to playing with my son so much that I was ready to get to the toy store and get all sorts of cool things to do with him. Strike one and strike two, rookie. First of all, play for a baby can be simply laying on their back discovering a mobile, looking at their new surroundings and learning about you. I didn't understand that until Kip arrived. Play evolves over time, but when you take the amount of stimulation into account that a baby is experiencing, baby steps are important to keep in mind when playing with your little spud. My next error was toys. Toys are great don't get me wrong. Babies don't need elaborate toys. Some might say kids, in general, don't need elaborate toys, but that is up to you and what you want for your kids. Basic is better in my book. I learned that with Kip. He has a butt load of toys that he has accumulated over the years. Most of the toys I bought were because they were things I thought were cool that he would enjoy. I feel like we, as dads, have our own memories that we take into the toy store. We remember what we liked and we want our kids to have the same experiences and memories that we did. That's all well and good, but keep one thing in mind. This little one is not you. They will have their own likes, dislikes, and interests.

In hindsight, I would hold off on a lot of toys because there are so many other ways to play that can provide the experiences we want for our kids. Again, don't get me wrong toys are great. We need to make sure the toys we choose for our kids have a purpose and are directed in the interests the kids have that we want to foster.

While your baby is a baby, play with them. Just remember, playing with a baby can be simply lying down on the ground with them and showing them blocks or stackable cups. You will be playing princesses and superheroes soon enough. Take this time to get to know your baby and allow them the chance to get to know their dad.

"Just play. Have fun. Enjoy the game." –Michael Jordan

BOTTLES VS. FOOD FOOD

Really? Am I writing about this?

Yup, I sure am.

Bottles will serve their purpose and so will real food.

Bottles will be the "go to" for a while, but I feel like you can start slowly bringing in real food as soon as you see fit. With Tad, he would totally watch us eat dinner and want what we had. He wanted real people food. Cool, game on, within reason.

Be ready for the mess. The mess is exactly that, a mess. Enjoy that time. It's awesome. Take pictures, realize you will need to clean up more and yes, again, it will be a mess. But, your little spud is learning how to eat.

Teach them.

I recall a time we had spaghetti with 8-month-old Tad. I strategically placed myself on the other side of the table for this event. My wife (who determined the meal and that Tad would eat spaghetti noodles at the table) was sitting right next to him. He loves to eat what we are eating and when it makes sense, I'm cool with that. Tad can totally handle spaghetti, but the fine motor is a work in progress. He grabs a handful and tries to carefully put it in his mouth. It's awesome. You have to enjoy this phase; I know I do because it goes by so fast. Several times during our meal, Tad would swipe his plate right off the table and his plate full of spaghetti with it. My wife would calmly collect the noodles and place them in front of Tad time after time.

You are teaching cause and effect as well as how to eat. Tad was learning so much during this time.

He knows he enjoys spaghetti, that's for sure. A 28-pound 8-month-old baby enjoys carbs? No way.

Every meal was pretty systematic with the Tadders. We usually began with something we fed him. That might be apples and pears we put through our Vitamix, mixed up with some rice cereal. From there, I try to get him something he can feed himself with, like Ritz crackers or graham crackers. After that, he always ends his meals with some bottle time. We know his routine and it works for us.

What will your routine be?

Kip was totally different that Tad. Kip is more of a grazer, always has been.

The big thing to keep in mind is the end goal. You want to get the nutrition into the baby. If your wife is breastfeeding or pumping, that is great. My wife pumped for 8 months with Kip and 6 months with Tad. That's just amazing dedication and discipline. If you are in that world, you need to stay on top of it or the baby will not have any food. With Tad, after 6 months, my wife told me she needed to be done. Who am I to tell her otherwise? It really doesn't affect me at all. Any mama willing to take on pumping or breastfeeding is a rock star.

Be mindful of that if your wife is willing to dedicate her time to creating food for your baby. It's her body, her schedule and her time that is coming into play. Guys really don't play a factor into it. That is unless, of course, you hear about no bake cookies assisting in the production of breast milk. Yup, they do.

When we were in a bit of a pinch for breast milk with Tad, I found myself up at 11:30 at night, looking up the recipe for the best no bake cookies. I got out all the ingredients and whipped up a double batch of those bad boys. I wish I could say they were just for my wife, but those things are awesome. I probably ate a whole batch myself.

Just like everything else you will read in these pages, the decision of what you will do is ultimately up to you and your wife. It's your life and your children. Do what you feel makes the most sense and what you are willing to stick to.

When it comes to feeding a baby, the decision is really up to the mama. Dad, stand back and let the mama bear handle this department. You are just on the sidelines. She is in the game. Like it or not, your nipples are useless in this game.

Yup, I just said that. That was awesome.

Lesson to be learned: You will figure out what plan of attack works best for feeding your baby. Respect the mamas that are pumping and breastfeeding. It takes time, patience and discipline. Honestly, even if a dude's nipples could make milk, we wouldn't have the discipline needed to keep it flowing.

LIVE LIKE BO

Our amazing day began in the harbor on Virgin Gorda, in the British Virgin Islands. It was there that we met Elton and Pops, the captain and the head mate on our ride for the day. The Pampered Pirate was a luxury yacht that my wife's Aunt Pat and Uncle Mike chartered for the day. Amazing is all I can say.

As we climbed aboard the boat, it was clear this was going to be a "Bo" day. A "Bo" day is a day that goes beyond in all ways. Bo days are pushed to the maximum level of awesome and fun. Extreme. Bo was my wife's cousin who knew how to make you smile, feel welcome and always have an amazing time.

We made our way out to sea and spent the day island hopping, snorkeling in caves, having run-ins with barracuda and jellyfish and feeling the amazing breeze ignite your soul. Yeah, it was that amazing. This was one of those days where you felt more alive than any other day you've lived.

For lunch, we stopped at a place called Willy T's. It's a floating restaurant near Norman Island in the British Virgin Islands. Crazy to see a boat converted into a restaurant in the middle of the water. The atmosphere was one of feeling all that it means to be free. Willy T's has 2 levels. Bo immediately took us to the top level. He points to the back of the boat, "...and that's where we jump off into the water." Jump off? I went over to take a took to see exactly how high up I would be hurling my grain fed butt into the water. The leap seemed gigantic. We had each had a few Heinekens, but nothing to make you feel silly enough to take the plunge.

Without hesitation, Bo ran the length of the boat and superman leaped off the back. I don't remember what I said at that moment, but it was definitely one of those, "holy balls" moments. My brother in law, Chip, was next; off he went, over the edge, happy as a clam. All of the sudden, I realized I was "next" in line. I had one of those, "you might not ever get this chance again" moments, so off I went. The fall off the side of the boat was beautiful, fast and intense. It was amazing. My wife took a picture of Bo, Chip and me in the water. We made a silly pose. Every time I see that picture, I smile. We made the jump several times while we were there. One time, Bo almost jumped right on top of a barracuda! Going out to lunch has never quite been the same since that day at Willy T's.

After lunch, we hopped over to another island. Rolling up to a Caribbean island beach on a luxury yacht with music blaring was awesome. Elton and Pops stayed on the boat, threw the anchor and some of us swam ashore. The beach was filled with people enjoying themselves, on their vacations from whatever lives they led. Here we were, just making a quick stop at their vacation destination. The beach was beautiful, but being able to swim back to the Pampered Pirate to head to another island was even cooler. Again, this was a "Bo day".

Our next stop was a small island in the British Virgin Islands called "Sandy Spit". It's an uninhabited island that's less than half an acre in size. Elton pulled up; we jumped off and walked around the sandy shores of Sandy Spit. It was crazy to think we were the only people on this little island, in the middle of this beautiful water. We made "sand angels" on the beach (it was winter and we all lived in areas that were covered with snow back home at the time). We were beginning to wrap up our day and you could tell everyone was just taking it all in.

On our way back to Virgin Gorda, I remember sitting at the front of the boat with my feet dangling over the side. Tamsen, Chip, Bo and I were all pretty much doing the same thing. Enjoying the end of an amazing day on the sea. The gorgeous water splashed our feet and the peaceful air blew through our hair. It was the closest thing to paradise anyone could experience on Earth.

Soon we arrived back in Virgin Gorda and started getting dressed for dinner. Dinner was an amazing end to a fantastic day.

This was one of those days I could talk about every day. I could go on and on about this one day. The air was easier to breathe and you just felt totally free.

Robert Keith Marshall.

Ever heard of him? Sadly, the answer is more than likely, no.

Robert Keith Marshall was my wife's cousin, who was more like a brother to her.

He was known by all who knew him as "Bo".

This dude was a rock star in every sense of the phrase. He was larger than life and hard to miss in person due to his height. The sweetest, kindest, brightest, funniest, most caring guy you could ever meet. A hero.

Bo was the kind of guy who would do anything for anyone, anytime. That was him and how he lived life. He lived life to its fullest, squeezing every little ounce out of each day, making the world a better place.

Bo gave his life so those he loved would be safe. So I could be a dad. So you could be a dad.

Why am I sharing this with you?

There are a lot of reasons.

We all have people we care about beyond words in our lives. Bo was one of those people. He still is. The morning we got the phone call from New York City to deliver the shocking news that Bo was dead was a day that changed our lives forever. Kip's Uncle Bo was gone. He never got to take Kip to a Rangers game. Aunt Pat and Uncle Mike's only son was gone. He never got to smile at them as he was standing at the altar to get married or to share his newborn son or daughter with them.

My wife, Tamsen lost a cousin by blood, but a brother by heart.

A young boy, who she saw grow up into one hell of an amazing man.

A national hero. Gone.

The loss of Bo changed how Tamsen and I see life. Life changed that day. We knew we needed to live each day to its absolute fullest. We needed to live more "Bo days".

I encourage you to live "Bo days" every day of your life. Bo was 24 when he died. I'm 40, but I am living more today than I have in the past, simply because I want to be more. I see the beautiful in the world. I try new things that are out of my comfort zone. I strive to be the best dad and husband I can be. I try to make other people better. I want more for my family. I want to live a life worth living.

As a dad, you have the amazing opportunity to be the BEST dad you possibly can. It's so easy to screw up priorities in our lives. Since Bo died, family has always been first for me. I don't know about you, but I cannot imagine leaving my boys, or my wife anytime soon. I have too much love to give them and I just want to experience life with them.

Each day is a gift. Wake up empowered and feeling good. You're a dad. Be the dad you know your little ones deserve.

We all have a choice.

Lesson to be learned: Live more "Bo days".

HELICOPTER VS. COMMON SENSE...THE GREAT DEBATE

There is no debate. Common sense should always win.

What exactly is a helicopter parent? Someone who is continually hovering over his or her kids?

Many times, I think people label other people as helicopter parents based on their perception. Everyone has his or her own perception and are always willing to share their opinion, whether you want it or not.

The other side of the helicopter parent is the absent-minded oblivious DB parent (A.M.O.D.B.). You know the type. In their own world, totally oblivious to what their kids are doing. Wake up! We all have our moments, but the goal is to minimize them. Live in the now they say. Whenever possible, try to keep the head out of the butt.

Obviously, the helicopter parent and the A.M.O.D.B. parent are extreme examples of the parenting spectrum.

Which will you be? Perhaps a combo platter of both?

Nah, not you.

You will be the parent who subscribes to the legendary, mythological, ever powerful skill know as common sense. Yes, for the low, low price of NOTHING, you too can use common sense in your parenting.

IF it looks dangerous, it probably is!

IF something seems wrong, it probably is!

IF something doesn't feel right, it probably isn't!

IF you smell poop, it probably is! (Go wipe that poopy butt!)

All kidding aside, you know right from wrong and what makes the most sense to you and your family. Go with that. We will all have moments that guide us into all of the above categories. The key is finding balance and consistency.

Common sense is a great approach when raising little ones, as well as life in general. However, as life has shown us, common sense is not always so common. It takes practice.

It's worth the practice. We're talking about your kids.

After all, we don't need any more DBs in the world.

What smells of common sense and works for your family is what is best for you. People will always be willing to lend their perspective on what they did when they had little kids. What they did was right for them. Some will try to sell you on the idea that the way they did things was the best way to handle each parenting situation. Maybe it was for them.

Take other's perspectives and advice with a rather large grain of salt. Use your common sense powers to filter what makes sense for you and what should be tossed in the diaper bin.

Lesson to be learned: Everyone will have advice on everything under the sun when it comes to how you should parent. Allow yourself the time to figure out what works best for you. You've got this.

TRICK OR TREAT TOOTLES MCGOO...

Do you remember any of your Halloween costumes from when you were a kid?

I can clearly remember being E.T. when I was in Kindergarten. Back then, you could get a costume in a rectangular box that includes a plastic mask (with the elastic string on the back to hold it to your face) and a plastic costume. Sometimes the costumes were made to look like the character or made you look like a billboard. It was all good. I loved the plastic costumes.

I remember being E.T. mainly because I really got into the character. I went around the classroom, leaving a trail of Reese's Pieces all over the floor. Once the trail was complete. I turned around and one by one picked them back up and ate them. The simple things in life were and are still awesome.

Do you remember any of your trick or treating experiences?

Mine are a compilation of memories, all fun and with friends. I always enjoyed Halloween, even though it seemed to rain most of the time here in Michigan. One year, I was a punk rocker (loved the 80's) and my mom helped me create a costume with a trash bag and duct tape. Throw a little blue hair coloring into the mix and you were all set.

Back then, things seemed so simple. Wow, that made me sound really old. Is 40 old? I hear it's the new 30.

What traditions are you going to create for your family, now that you are a dad?

Getting pumpkins from the local pumpkin patch?

Hayrides and corn mazes?

Throwing a neighborhood Halloween party for the kids?

Dressing up the family based on a theme?

It's totally up to you.

Year after year, I try to remember this is a magical time for Kip. Soon, Tad will be joining in on the magic that is Halloween. We have a pretty good neighborhood for trick or treating. Most of the neighbors participate and we don't have any creepers where we live. If we want to invite friends over to our house to trick or treat, that base is covered.

We started a tradition when Kip was 2. There is a family farm about 30 minutes from where we live. They have a pumpkin train (orange barrels, on their side with wheels attached, pulled by a tractor), petting zoo, corn maze, pumpkin patch, donuts and cider. This has become a fun time for our family. Kip wears his costume (one of his many) and we have a great time.

This year, we actually looked into taking a Disney Halloween Cruise. Kip loves Mickey and we thought it could be a fun way to take him on his first cruise experience. If we go, the plan is to have Kip dress up as Sully and Tad as Mike Wazowski. Awesome, right? *Holy crap* that would be awesome!

What about you? Are you going to dress up with your kids? Are you going to hand out candy?

No matter what you decide, make sure you do something that will be memorable for you and your kids, as everyone grows older.

When you get involved, you can't go wrong.

Lesson to be learned: Challenge your comfort zone and have fun with your kids on Halloween. It's once a year. Go all out.

PB&J = BUTT LOADS OF $?

Has anyone ever stopped to tell you that you have an ATM machine between your ears?

You do.

Let me explain.

- Do you have any interests?
- Do you have any hobbies you are extremely passionate about?
- Do you have particular skills that you are really good at?
- Do you have an education or training that you needed to begin your career?

The answer to most (or all) of these is a resounding YES!

It's called intellectual property. Yes, my wife is a lawyer and yes that is totally something a lawyer would say. Intellectual property is anything you know. Does everyone else know what you know? No, they don't.

Ok, so where the heck does peanut butter and jelly tie into this? Well, six years ago, when Kip was born, my wife recently graduated from law school (with honors, yup totally bragging about my amazing wife) and passed the

State of Michigan Bar Exam (first time, again bragging). She had a tough decision to make.

- Work for a traditional firm with insanely long hours?
- Go work for the IRS in Detroit during the week and come home on the weekends?
- Work for the legal department of a company or business?
- Go back into the collegiate trademark licensing business, but this time with a law degree? (What she did before law school)

The answer to ALL of these was an overwhelming *OH HELL NO!*

She (we) did not like the idea of her missing so much time with our new baby boy. But, law school is essentially another mortgage of debt and she knew she wanted to practice law. My wife created her own law firm that she was able to begin, grow, build and transform into what she wanted a law firm to be. It was awesome. During the course of this adventure, she began to help clients take what they already knew, create a product they were able to share with the world and make money for their family. Sweet deal right? On top of that, she was also able to show them how to protect what they created since she has the legal knowledge to do that. So many people are only interested in legal when they are already up the creek without a paddle. Always a good idea to keep a couple paddles in the boat with you.

Tamsen (my wife) has created a program called PB&J Course Design. It essentially allows anyone to take what they know (and love), share it with the world and make extra money for their family.

The super rad part was this past summer. I have always been Mr. Skeptic guy when it came to online anything. Tamsen encouraged me to think about an idea that she could use to take me through her PB&J system.

One day, I was on my way home from the gym and I thought about a part of my job that I enjoy above all else. For the past sixteen years, I've taught sixth grade and I really enjoy helping kids learn how to create class presentations. Presenting is one of the king daddy fears of the kids I work with and probably most people in general.

So, I get home and tell her I had an idea. I was really excited. She set things up and in 37 minutes, she showed me how to create multiple products that would allow me to sell what I knew online and to make extra money in the process. It was freaking amazing!

Not only did she show me how to create a course with what I knew, she changed how I view the online world.

Going through the process changed my mindset. I felt free in a way. It was really cool.

I went from:

I'm a teacher, that's all I do. Online course creation is your thing, not mine.

TO

I'm a teacher; it's part of what I do. I think I could create something online.

TO

I teach and I enjoy it, but it's not all I do. I know how to create online products and I am excited to learn more!

It was insane. The really amazingly awesome part was my wife and I created a book related to this system after I went through the process. Easy As PB&J is a book that takes you through our adventure. It also takes you through the rationale behind the book and the step-by-step process you need to begin taking what you know and cashing in.

Tamsen and I have a passionate mission. We want all families to be able to redefine how work is done. We crave the day when all families have more time together and more money to live the life they want to live.

I would encourage you to rethink how you view "work" and how it impacts your life with your family.

Lesson to be learned: A dog is never too old to learn new tricks. I'm tagging you, you're it, it's your turn to find *YOUR* awesome and get it out into the world!

YOU LOVE _____, WILL THEY?

I love hockey.

I love going to the gym.

I love being near water.

I love coffee.

I love my family.

We all have the things we love that simply bring us oodles of joy. The hope for some parents is that their kids will love what they love.

Kip and I have been going up to Traverse City for the NHL Prospect Tournament for the past few years. Every year we go, he seems to enjoy it more and more. Last year when we went, it was so much fun. He was 5 and a total clown. The tournament is in a smaller rink; so all the seats are good. Here we are in Michigan and the guy is sporting his New York Rangers jersey, totally awesome.

My wife's family lives in NYC and they are New York Ranger's fans. Despite my love for my Detroit Redwings, I love that Kip likes the Rangers. It's his thing. He has a connection to the Rangers through my wife's family and probably always will. That's pretty cool. So, here we are, at the rink, sitting in the stands. He says to me, "Dad, do you think a player will give me a puck?" I told him we would try, but it can be really hard for the players to give kids pucks when they are getting ready for a game. These are prospects; after all, they are trying to impress scouts for the NHL teams in attendance. They aren't going to be giving my son pucks.

Or are they?

The players hit the ice for the first game. Kip is right up against the glass, taking it all in. A player skates right in front of him, tosses him a puck. Happy boy. Five minutes go by and another player sees him, skates over and tosses him puck number 2. After the first period, the players are shuffling off the ice and a prospect spots him. He walks over and tosses him puck number 3. Kip comes up to me, happy as a pig in poo with his new collection of galvanized rubber. We put those in our backpack and head to the other sheet of ice at the rink to watch the game going on over there. That game was just getting ready to begin and we caught the tail end of the warm-ups. You guessed it. As Kip was down by the glass, a player tosses him puck number 4. Later on that day, the Redwings were playing the Blackhawks and a Chicago player gave him another puck. In all, I think he walked away with like 6 pucks.

That experience was just cool. It was just a trip Kip and I took. The trip was totally based on one of my main interests, but Kip has told me several times that he likes watching hockey with me because he knows it makes me happy. That's awesome. I know he enjoys it as well, but that's a pretty sweet boy.

Flipping the coin the other way, Kip has taken a liking to baseball. I'm not the biggest fan of the sport, but when we signed him up for t-ball, he asked me if I would help coach his team. How could I say no? Well, I could have, but what do I want his memories to be? Do I want him to have memories of being on a team while his dad was watching? Nah, I want the memories to include me talking to him at first base, in the batter's box and in the dug out. That's the good stuff and he will always remember it. Again, not my interest at all, but he loves it.

So, what's your uber passion? Are you a hunter or fisherman? Football? Basketball? Golf? No matter what you absolutely love, there are no guarantees that your kids will love what you do. That doesn't mean you can't include them. Kip enjoys hockey because it's something he does with me. Bottom line. I enjoyed coaching t-ball because I knew it meant a lot to him.

When your kids find what they love, make sure you return the favor of sharing in their passion as well.

Lesson to be learned: Always include your kids in your interests. Sharing what you love is important to them.

SLEEP?

Cue Master Yoda ... soon will I rest? Yes. Forever sleep.

You may wish for forever sleep but for-never sleep is more like it!

Once your baby is here you more than likely have a better understanding of why sleep deprivation is a common and widely used form of torture. All of the sudden, a solid 4-hour chunk of sleep just sounds so dreamy. Don't worry solid chunks of sleep will come back to your world ... just not right now.

Before kids, my wife and I were not night owls by any means. As I am typing this, it's 8:27 p.m. and my house is done for the day. The lights are off and everyone is asleep. I know we go to sleep earlier now, as parents, simply because it makes sense to get the rest when the kids do and also when our body craves it.

How will sleep look for your family once the baby arrives? Maybe you already know the plan or are already in the midst of experimenting how to make sure everyone gets his or her rest.

I can tell you from experience, having a baby certainly keeps you on your toes, even when you are supposed to be sleeping. When Kip was a baby, he did not care for his crib. He would scream and scream and scream. Some people will tell you to let the baby cry it out. That just wasn't how we wanted to handle it.

The stress hormones released when a baby is going through that just doesn't jive with my wife and I. That's us. It might not be you, but it's how we rolled. Many nights, Kip had ear infections, teeth coming in or wasn't feeling well. We became so accustomed to holding him upright during the night (to keep the pressure off his head while he laid flat) that it became normal. Many nights, as Kip got older, he would come to our room and want to sleep with us. Again, that was fine with us, but it's not for everyone. You have to know what's best for you and your family and stick with it. Do what you feel is right, that's what matters.

Tad is completely different than Kip when it comes to sleep. He is a smiley guy who likes being around people. He wants to see what's going on and who's in the room. When it comes to sleep, he wants to be alone. He loves his crib and does a great job of rubbing his eyes to cue us when he is toast. Tad has a small stuffed animal he loves to snuggle with, but that's it. Due to his silent reflux (and teething), he was getting 2-3 hour chunks of sleep at night. Tad did not sleep through the night until he was a little over 1 year old. I made a deal with my wife early on that if I took the night shift, I would go to the gym early in the morning. I just wanted to make sure I could get to the gym. She gets an opportunity of a solid night of sleep; I hang with Tad man (getting up 3-5 times during the night) and get to go to the gym. Sound like a crazy trade off? Makes sense to me and that's all that matters.

Just like everything else that goes along with being a new parent, do what makes sense to you. There are so many little pieces to the puzzle, sleep just happens to be a pretty important one. You need your rest. Everyone does. Get it in a way that allows you to sleep well at night.

Lesson to be learned: Coffee is your friend. Seriously though, have a sleep plan. Trade on and off nights with your wife or be able to read when one or the other of you needs a solid night of rest. There will be nights where you are both up all night. Have a plan to try to ensure one or both of you has the chance to get the best sleep you can.

DAMN YOU, FRUIT SNACKS

Gel globs of hell.

Fruit snacks are a dirty, dirty whore. They are all that is evil. Pure evil.

Ok, rant complete. Why my intense disdain for fruit snacks? Well, it's pretty much my fault and my wife's fault, but fruit snacks are not innocent either.

As Kip was growing up, he began to have his teeth grow in. Teething in of itself wasn't that bad for Kip. At the time, he loved fruit snacks. So did we. They were cheap, fun and easy for Kip to eat. Before bed, he would usually try to get a snack in. His choice, fruit snacks.

Ok, let's pause right there. Think about what fruit snacks are. Gel globs of hell. That's not in the ingredients, but that's a summary of what they are. Hop on Google and read the ingredients on a pack of fruit snacks. Go ahead, I'll wait.

Now, go get a little package of fruit snacks from your cupboard, you know you have them. Open them up and eat them. Notice anything? Sticking to your teeth a bit?

Yes, yes they do. So, Kip was eating fruit snacks before bed for, well, I don't know how many days, weeks or months.

Dentist appointment was coming up. I'm wondering how he's going to do, sitting in the chair and all of that. We go to the appointment and the hygienist begins to look in Kip's mouth. She stops, looks at me and proceeds to tell me he has a large number of cavities and it would take multiple appointments to fix them all.

Gut punch followed up with the junk shot.

I felt awful. I felt like the worst dad ever.

The dentist recommended we go to a pediatric dentist, as they would be able to better meet our needs. A DENTIST DIDN'T WANT TO TOUCH THIS WITH A TEN FOOT POLE! It was that bad. When a health professional basically turns you away, even though you have great insurance and the service you need will bring in a nice bill, that's crazy. But, that's where we were.

This sucked.

We went to the pediatric dentist and they examined his mouth. From there, the dentist sat down with my wife and I to tell us she was going to have to remove 2 of Kip's teeth because they were so decayed, put a crown on another and filled another 6-8 cavities. Holy balls. Holy freaking balls.

Worst parents ever part 2, the return of yeah we suck.

The dentist asked us about our routine for Kip's teeth and what he was eating, particularly at night. Damn you fruit snacks! She went on to tell us fruit snacks are one of the worst things to eat at night because they stick to your teeth. If you don't brush well enough, they are sitting on your teeth all night, chomping away at your teeth.

Kip had to go to the hospital for the dental procedure. They felt it best to put him under and the hospital was the best place to do that for safety reasons.

Again, worst parent ever part 3, to say you suck is too kind.

He made it through everything, was a little sore, but he did great.

Kip's a rock star.

The price of eating fruit snacks and not brushing well cost us about what it would have cost to go to Disney for a few days.

What's the point of this story? Get on those teeth early and often. Watch the snacks you make available at night to your kids. Most importantly, go visit a pediatric dentist to schedule appointments as soon as they feel your little one is ready.

Damn fruit snacks.

Lesson to be learned: Boycott fruit snacks. They are little globs of hell.

SCRUB A DUB DUB, A SHOWER OR THE TUB?

How about both?

I don't know about you, but sometimes a shower is just what the doctor ordered at the beginning of the day or the end of the day (most days both). Then again, on those days where you don't feel well or are a bit sore, a soak in a tub (especially a jet tub) feels great.

Your baby is no different. Most people prefer to scrub a dub in the tub. Both of my boys love the shower. Kip loved the water on his back and Tad likes to stick his tongue out and feel the water. On the other hand, they both like baths as well. We have a jet tub, Tad enjoys trying to eat the bubbles and Kip doesn't like having the jets on at all. He does, however, enjoy watching a show on an iPad while in the tub. Baths generally take longer, but that isn't necessarily a bad thing.

Once again, you will know your baby and kids best. They will do a great job of guiding you in this area. I am very thankful that both of my boys enjoy the water. They always have.

Preference aside, some days a shower or the tub is a need based on the situation. For example, if Tad has a stage 5 blowout of a diaper and he's a complete mess, and then decides to do the running man on the changing pad, I might have a need for an impromptu shower. Poo covered junk can lead to poo covered hands which can lead to a poo covered face, or worse yet, poo in the mouth. Yes, head for the shower folks.

Another time a shower might just do the trick is if your little one isn't feeling well. With Kip, the shower was magic for calming him down when he didn't feel well, during teething or when his head hurt from an ear infection. It's pretty much been the same for my man Tad. He calms right down in the shower. It's almost like a reset button. You can almost feel their little bodies chilling out as the water softly hits their skin.

As far as the tub goes, neither of my guys liked the kid tubs. I can't say I blame them. They are all pretty lame. When Kip was a baby, I went in the tub with him. Great chance to play with bath toys and get him familiar with the idea of being in the water. Now, with Tad, we do the same thing. He enjoys his bath toys and trying to catch the water as it pours out of the faucet.

Either way, you really can't go wrong. I know many people are anti-shower for the fear of dropping the baby. I get it and if that makes you nervous, stick to the tub. Find your own way that feels comfortable to you. That's what's important.

At the end of the day, you have to be cool with all of these little decisions. It's your life and your experience with your little person.

Lesson to be learned: Your kids will need to get clean one-way or the other. Find the way that makes the most sense to you.

TOKEN ECONOMY

Did you get an allowance when you were a kid?

I remember my big money maker was mowing the yard. My grandma paid me $5 once a week to do the yard. It was a small yard, usually took around 30 minutes. Aside from the money, I enjoyed visiting my grandma. She was one of those people you just liked visiting, always fun to talk to. It's not every day that you have a sweet old lady cursing about something in Polish. That's just awesome. My grandma also kept an amazing stash of assorted chocolate bars in her fridge. That was awesome as well.

When I was in elementary school, around third grade, G.I. Joe was big. Therefore, after mowing the yard, my mom always drove me to the local dime store, where I would attempt to find either a new addition to my G.I. Joe army or a new Cobra soldier. Times were good, simple. I also learned early on that money was not as easy to earn, as it is to spend.

Enter the token economy.

Since Kip was rather little, maybe as early as 2, we have used a token economy with him. We saw rather quickly how he expected to get something every time we went to the store. That had to be addressed in a way that would help him understand how money actually works. So, we came up with age appropriate jobs that would allow him to help around the house and earn tokens. The tokens are essentially poker chips from the dollar store, but they work great. We stick with one color. Early on, when Kip completed a task, he got a token for his jar. The value of each token is up to you. Early on, we made a token worth fifty cents. Whenever we would go to the store, especially the toy store, Kip was always curious to see what he could afford. We used a pencil pouch for him to keep his tokens in and he took his money with him to the store. Whenever he found something he wanted, we would count how much he had and compare it with the price. It really gave us a good chance to practice counting and trying to explain the value of one number compared to another.

Fast forward to today. Kip is 6 and his system has changed a bit. He now has 3 different cups filled with 5 Popsicle sticks. He has one cup for the morning, one for the afternoon and one for the evening. Each Popsicle stick has a chore or task Kip needs to complete. If all 5 sticks are completed within a certain amount of time, he gets one token. He uses his tokens for iPad time (1 token = 30 minutes) mainly or he can save them for bigger things like going to the movies or to Dave and Buster's.

It takes some work to get kids on a system that they will buy into, but I think it's worth it. Find a system that works for you, tinker with it if you have to, but have a system.

My wife is amazing at systems like this and other time savers. She loves creating solutions where there are bumps in the road. That's a pretty good skill to have when sailing the waters of parenthood.

Lesson to be learned: Good to have a system to help kids understand the value of money. The earlier you can bring this in, the better.

BE THE TICKLE MONSTER

Do you remember any special games your dad played with you?

You either do or you don't. There really isn't any middle ground.

I think about Jim Carey in Liar Liar with his "claw" game he plays with his son.

For Kip and I, it's the tickle monster.

The tickle monster started when Kip was really young. That dude is probably the most ticklish person in the world. Under his arms, legs, belly, back, he's just ticklish. More importantly, he loves being tickled.

Enter the tickle monster.

Kip loves playing games, as most kids do. He loves being chased, caught and tickled. Add in a little character development and you have yourself a game, a game that Kip will remember for a long time. In fact, he has already started playing tickle monster with his little brother, Tad. More than likely, one day, I will see Kip playing tickle monster with his own kids, when I am a grandpa.

Wow, that was weird to type, me being a grandpa.

As they say, time stops for no one and it will be here before you know it.

So, right now, our job is to make our own games that we know our kids will love.

Tickle monster is the game Kip will remember. He loves playing it.

I'm proud to be the tickle monster.

Who will you be?

Lesson to be learned: Have fun with your kids! Make games that bring joy into your home.

SOME ASSEMBLY REQUIRED

Christmas morning. You did your job as Santa and the stage is set for an amazing, magical morning. Good job.

Then you remember. Rut roh, there were a bunch of toys you remember wrapping that needed to be put together. No big deal, you tell yourself.

Your kids wake up and see the amazing piles of joy under the tree. Excitement fills the room. The presents start to lose their wrapping paper and smiles fill the faces of the little ones.

Then, your kids come up to you with a few of their new toys. "Dad, can you put this together?" Of course, you can, right? So, you dig into the first thing. You need a screwdriver, some batteries and a bit of patience. Not only that, but your kids keep asking you if you are done, yet?

Could this yuck/blah feeling be avoided? Yes. Yes, it can.

A couple years ago, I had this situation play out in my house. Kip unwrapped all kinds of presents that needed to be put together. It's no big deal, but if I could reduce the amount I had to put together, that would be great. The way I reduced what I had to put together Christmas morning was simple.

- Before you wrap a present, notice if it needs to be put together.
- Put the toy together.
- Wrap the empty box.
- Boom. Done.

Kip had one of those motorized vehicles given to him one year. We knew he would love it, but opening a box of parts is kind of a bummer. So, I put the vehicle together, hid it downstairs and wrapped the empty box. When he opened the box, I had it all made, so he could hop right on and enjoy it.

I went through this ninja process with quite a number of toys the past few years. I know it makes the whole day more enjoyable when there is less stress.

This is just another one of those simple things that can help you out a bit in the role of being a dad.

Lesson to be learned: Some assembly required can happen before a present is unwrapped.

TRAVEL TIME WITH THE SPUD

We love to travel. Getting out and living in the world is a big part of how we live our #vacationinglife.

Living in Michigan, we are about 40 minutes from Lake Michigan, about 5 1/2 hours from Mackinac Island, 3 hours from Chicago and 11 1/2 hours from Princeton, New Jersey.

Quite a random list, hey?

Lake Michigan is one of our favorite places to spend time. We are very fortunate to live so close to such a beautiful area with so many beaches and awesome places to eat, near the water. Travel time to Lake Michigan is around 40 minutes, not a long drive at all. In fact, during the week, I can call my wife and see if she would like to do a picnic dinner at the beach. Any night of the week can be filled with sand, kids playing in the water and a gorgeous sunset. Yeah buddy, 40 minutes for a peaceful winding down to a day is awesome.

Mackinac City and Mackinac Island are places I have been visiting since I was really young. My dad always went up there when he was a kid as well. He was even up there while they were building the bridge. Such a subtle area, but

I just enjoy it. We can drive up there early in the morning (5 1/2 hours) and catch one of the earlier ferries to the island. Now, as a dad, I love taking Kip up there. Horses all over the island, riding bikes around the island and getting some fudge. It's just a great little get away that's not crazy far away. The travel time is quite a bit longer than Lake Michigan, but it's a good chance to get away. We usually go at least once a year.

Chicago is just one of those cities people like to visit. My brother in law lives there as well. It makes sense for us to go to Chicago now and then to visit my boy's uncle and hang out in the big city. My wife took Kip on a visit a couple years ago and they used the Amtrak train. That was great. Kip loved the train ride and my wife didn't have to worry about driving. It's a 3-hour drive, but if you can have your kids enjoying the ride there a bit more, that makes it more of an adventure.

Princeton, New Jersey probably seems like the oddest destination on this list. Well, my wife's family lived there a few years ago and we took Kip on his first major road trip to visit. Around a 750-mile drive, we broke it up into a couple of days. Definitely, the longest road trip we have taken with kids. This trip taught me one thing, 750 miles is not meant to be driven. Since that time, my wife's family has moved to New York City (Manhattan). We have visited them there as well, but we flew.

By far, my favorite place we have gone since having kids has been Disney World. We flew, stayed at the Contemporary Resort and we had an amazing time. Kip and I talk about going back all the time. We had a blast.

No matter what trips you decide to take, remember they are meant to be an adventure. Have fun. Pace yourself and remember that you set the tone for your family. Take breaks. If you see something cool along your journey, stop and check it out.

Lesson to be learned: Travel on dad. Get out and about. Live.

LITTLE HELPERS

Kids want to help, they always do. It's cool when you're little to help your mom and dad. Do you remember wanting to help your mom or dad in the grocery store? How about washing the car? Anything that involves using the ladder? You bet.

It seems, as kids grow older, they just want to do the "fun" things. For example, right now, Kip loves washing the car with me. He has his own scrubber and is a great hose man. It's just fun. Kip also likes doing a little gardening, just as long as I am doing it with him. He recently got his own gardening gloves, which he thinks are awesome. He will totally help me weed the yard, as long as I am right there next to him. He's not quite ready for me to have him do one area while I work on another. I'm cool with that. It's kind of nice on a Saturday to have him help me weed the yard. You never know what will come up in our conversations. Anything from superheroes to his latest ideas of a craft he wants to create. It's nice to just talk. Good practice, opening up that pipeline for later ages when it might not be as easy to talk about something.

The goal with your little helpers is to always have something they can help you with. Something you are cool with letting go. Kip likes spraying the windows and I wipe them off. He's helping in his own way.

How will you let your kids help out?

You might not know right now and that's totally ok. As your kids grow, they will start to notice what you and your wife do around the house. Whatever mom and dad do is usually pretty cool. At least part of what they do can be cool, like Kip spraying the windows to help me out.

Allowing your kids to help out is very important to them. It lets them know how much mom and dad do. It also gives them a chance to help out where ever they can to help free up some mom and dad time to do something a little more fun.

Lesson to be learned: Let the kids help.

SWEET DIAPER BAG DUDE!

So, when you are at the baby store going down the list of things you are registering for, did you get yourself a diaper bag?

Yes? Cool.

No? Why not?

Take a look at that section of the baby store. The majority of the bags are geared towards the moms. That's all well and good, but what if you are out and about with your little spud? Do you want to carry mom's bag around?

This is totally up to you. No judgment here.

Well, maybe a little.

When it comes to being a dad, it's all about decisions that make sense to you. That's all that matters.

My wife enjoys bags that she can use for multiple things. With Kip, I got her a Kate Spade diaper bag that she knew she would also use as a purse when she no longer needed a diaper bag. With Tad, I went with Orla Kiely's leaf patterned bag because I knew she loved it and she would use it as a purse as well. Get your wife something jazzy. Splurge a bit. She will love it.

But, what about you?

Do you want your own bag?

C'mon, you know you do.

Anyway, I did. My wife was all about me getting my own diaper bag. Now, there are diaper bags geared towards dads, but once that phase is gone, I knew I wouldn't be using that bag for anything else.

So, what do you get?

You get a sweet backpack. That's what you get. I went to the North Face store and got something that I knew would work as a diaper bag, but also something I would use a number of ways once the diaper bag phase was over.

I thought it was kind of cool to get something just for me. When I took Kip anywhere, just him and I, I could throw my bag under the stroller and know I had everything I needed without feeling like flower power.

So, go on dad. Get yourself a diaper bag. Make it something that makes you happy. Go olive drab, slate, or charcoal and make sure it has all sorts of buckles with a sweet logo. Sorry, got carried away there.

It's just another part of being a dad. You might as well treat yourself and enjoy it.

Lesson to be learned: You should get some baby gear as well!

WHAT? NO HOCKEY?!

Hobbies will more than likely adjust and change a bit upon the arrival of your little spud. You will figure out a way to continue to make them happen if you really want to.

Before Kip was born, I played hockey a couple times a week and went to the gym 3-4 times a week. I think I was completely oblivious to the changes that were in store for me when he arrived. Once Kip was here, things just changed. It certainly wasn't a bad change, but my priorities just switched up a bit. I really didn't care if I played hockey as much. I played now and then. First, it was once a week, then once every couple weeks until it just dwindled away. Wow, as I am writing this, it sounds so depressing. That's not my intent at all. I'm totally cool with the hockey time I have. I actually found a great group of guys that run a 6 a.m. skate at a rink near the school where I teach. It's on Tuesday mornings and I can leave the house before anyone is awake. It works for everyone. If I feel the need to play hockey, that's an option that makes sense to me.

When Tad arrived, the change was there once again. My Tuesday morning skate still works out just fine. But, just like when Kip was born, my desire to play hockey has just decreased. It could be that I'm getting older, my aches and pains are more constant or I just like being home with my boys. I'm here to tell you, I just like being home with my boys. I still go play hockey now and then, but life changes and so do your priorities and passions.

What about you? What's your hobby you once lived for? Even though your free time has been rearranged a bit, there is still time for you to do what you love to do. There's always a way.

Find your 6 a.m. ice time and make it work.

It's always important to have time for our individual passions.

Lesson to be learned: Change is not a bad thing. You are in control of how you use the time you have.

THE STORE

Some people dread the store. We don't. We just don't. It's not a big deal for us. Before we had kids, we were the kind of people who enjoyed going to home stores to find new ways to make our home "ours". We just enjoyed it.

When Kip came along, we just needed to think things through a bit more. Younger kids are probably the easiest to take into the store. They are in awe of the lights, the sights, and the sounds. They are so distracted; they aren't sure what they are even looking at. As your kids get older, they become more aware.

Enter, the toy aisle. At some point, Kip became aware that most stores had a specific spot where they had a wide variety of toys. It was like he had some sort of toy radar and he could sense the presence of them. At first, we just took him down the aisles. He was cool with it, handled it well. Then, he upped the experience by wanting to go back to a certain aisle to see something again. From there, he started "wanting" things.

As the toy aisle experience grew for Kip, we began to set guidelines. We would give him a certain amount of time (say 5 minutes) and set the timer on our phone so he knew when the time was up. He became quite aware that he needed to keep moving. We also started coming up with a money system for him to earn tokens for helping around the house. Basic things that taught the idea that work could result in money. When we went to the store, he would take his tokens with him and when he found something he wanted, we would count his "monies" to see if he had enough. More times than not, he chose things that were out of his budget and that brought up the idea of saving.

We got to the point where I got very brave. I worked up the courage to take Kip to the toy store. Yes, you read that right, the toy store. Before we would go in, we had a game plan chat. We would see how much money we had, if we were just looking that day or if we had something, in particular, we wanted to find. I found that laying the ground rules before entering the land of toy overwhelm made a huge difference for Kip. We even came up with taking pictures of cool toys on daddy's phone to share with grandma, grandpa, and Santa. Brilliant!

Now, with two little awesomes, most of the time, we bring in Tad's stroller that has Kip's "piggyback" board that he can ride on. We are kinda sorta moving to the cart, which is cool because Kip can sit right next to Tad. This is so fun to watch. They almost entertain each other at this point. Win and win for everyone.

Do not fear taking your kids into the store. Based on my experience, having a game plan and explaining what the purpose of the visit is, helps a great deal. Give the kids jobs to help with the family's adventure. I always give Kip the list and a pen to scratch off when we find things we need. He eats that stuff up.

You know your kids best. You will find the ways to involve them in a way that will make the trip to the store more enjoyable for everyone.

Lesson to be learned: Game plans help make the trip to the store more manageable for everyone.

GET OUT AND ABOUT

There are a lot of theories on getting a baby out into the world and the correct time lines for doing just that.

You can read and hear many opinions that range from getting them out in public as soon as possible to keep them home in a calm environment.

I'm not here to tell you which way to roll with this area, just taking a moment to talk about it to perhaps lend some perspective.

When Kip was born, we really didn't go out that much. I think it had more to do with us being exhausted. My wife was in labor for him for 47 hours and really not knowing what to do. I can recall the first time I was going to take him for a walk around the block in his sweet new stroller (the Uppababy Vista, badass baby wheels). We literally got 3 houses away and he was screaming. Being the rookie I was, I quickly turned back around and headed for home. Adorable. Simply precious, when I look back on it.

When Tad was born, he wasn't even a week old and we were at an outside ice skating rink downtown. Kip and I were ice-skating while my wife had Tad bundled up in his stroller. I was in such a different mindset with Tad than I was with Kip.

Mindset is huge with this topic amongst others. Again, each kid is their own unique little person who will have their own tolerances, likes, dislikes, etc.

On Kip's final day of preschool, we took him to Dave and Buster's to celebrate. Kip loves that place. Tad, on the other hand, was in stage 5 overwhelm. The lights, the sounds, the atmosphere was just a bit much for a baby to handle. He hung in there for a bit, then it was clear, we should be heading out the door. The funny thing is, my wife can't stand the place either. Kip and I are having a blast. The sounds, lights, atmosphere are too much for my wife as well. Some places just affect different people in different ways.

Tad is a pretty chill dude. He is pretty easy to read most of the time. We didn't know this right off the bat, but once we got him home, he quickly showed us how he works, and what he needs. For instance, we got home after he was born on Christmas Eve. Perfect timing for Santa to still be able to make an appearance. In our family, we do our family presents on Christmas Eve at my home. So, the day we got back from the hospital, we had my family over. They did all the cooking, prepared everything, that wasn't a big deal. The part that threw Tad off was the amount of people over and the atmosphere in our house. It's usually quite calm, even with Kip playing superheroes or working on his ninja skills. When our company was over Tad kind of shut down. He closed his eyes and "slept" while everyone was over. Now, keep in mind, this little guy is only a few days old. Once everyone left, he opened his eyes and stayed awake for a while. He taught us that he needed a chill environment and that the change in energy when a lot of people are around was a bit much for him.

We never really shy away from taking our boys anywhere. You will know your kids best. For instance, if we are planning on going to the pool and Tad is rubbing his eyes before we leave, one of us stays home with him so he can rest. That saves us from taking a tired baby to the pool and still gets Kip his swim time.

Our city hosts an event called Art Prize. It's an art competition where venues throughout the city host entries from all over the world. Hundreds of entries in all sorts of cool places in our downtown, it's pretty cool, to say the least. We took the boys down for this event that occurs each September. Kip and Tad love being downtown. So many people, sights, bridges you can walk over and just so much life. We spent about 3 hours just wandering around the downtown area looking at the art and enjoying a beautiful Michigan fall day. The children's museum happened to be on our route, so we spent some time there as well. Again, no reason to fear taking the kids out, just important to make sure you have your bases covered.

As you get to know your baby (and your kids), you will no doubt realize that they all have certain "tells" that you will be able to read best because you are their dad. You will know your little people better than anyone.

Trial and error is one of the best ways to figure some of this stuff out. You don't know until you try.

One of my very good friends told me when I was a new father that as soon as you figure out something about your kids, they change the rules on you. I have found that to be a truth in fatherhood.

Keep on your toes and roll with the flow.

Get out there and show your kids their world.

Lessons to be learned: Live.

CAR VS. MINIVAN VS. SUV

One of the many things you will not see on the baby registration list.

The vehicle.

Oh balls, not a minivan, right?

What are you going to choose? Maybe you already have?

When Kip was born, we had a Honda CR-V. It was a great little SUV that did the job at the time. My wife drove that and I had a Honda Accord. Yes, a Honda family. They get crazy good family vehicle ratings and they lease out well (I like a new car every 3 years). Call me a snob. I'm the guy always driving a new car, Cheerios in the back seat and all.

When Tad was born, we chose to go with the Honda Odyssey minivan. Yes, a Honda again. That van is awesome.

Holy crap! Did I just write that?! "That van is awesome?" I must be mutating into something else.

I was the guy who was never going to own a van. I despised the van. I was revolted at the mere presence of a van on the road. They were disgusting creations that looked like loaves of bread meandering down the road.

Now, I love my loaf of bread.

With two kids, it's a total no-brainer. A van is great for everything from going to the store, to heading to the beach or going on vacation. You are covered. There is a ton of room, easy to clean and a nice ride.

Done and done.

Or is it?

You might be saying, "Not a minivan. Not me. Never."

As I said, I was in that club as well, until I drove my van. One drive was all it took. We loaded all the boy's things in and away we went. The only thing we struggled with was silver or truffle colored. (I know, I said truffle to describe a vehicle, sorry about that)

I always thought I would be the SUV guy. All wheel drive, sweet rims, a higher ride and all the awesome that goes along with so many of those gas guzzlers out there today.

I was mistaken.

Do your research. Test drive. Find something that functionally works the best for you and your family.

As my wife always says, "this is not a forever vehicle". She claims that every phase of life has a vehicle that makes sense. Right now, the minivan makes the most sense for us.

The funny thing is, I like it!

I play hockey, go to the gym and drink beer. My man card is still intact.

Did I mention it has sliding doors!?

Lesson to be learned: There is a vehicle for every stage of life. Your first car had a purpose (freedom). Your daddy ride also has a purpose and that purpose is to make your life easier. You can still get your satellite radio to listen to hockey.

DAYCARE DILEMMA

To daycare or not to daycare…

Depending on your personal situation, this might take care of itself or it could be something you are stressing over.

What happens when maternity leave is over?

Does mom go back to work or stay home?

You might already have this planned out, but if you don't, no worries. This is something parents go back and forth on all the time. Day care is not only expensive but leaving your baby, toddler or children in general with someone that is not you can be a bit stressful.

With Kip, we started off at a place some friends had a glowing experience with. It happened to play out that way for us as well. Drop off in the morning still sucked. Kip did not want me to leave and was a mess most mornings when I left him. Not a great way to start off your day. Leaving your little boy at a strange place to go to work. Hearing him cry as you walk away. That sucked. But, every day when I picked him up at the end of my workday, he was happy and had great things to talk about.

After Kip had grown a bit, he had to change rooms to a more age appropriate room. My wife and I did not care for the first few impressions of the teacher in the room and the vibe she was putting out. It was clear that this would not be a fit for Kip and it wasn't going to happen.

Before I go any further, you might be thinking I sound like someone who is trying to protect his little boy. You're damn right I am. You should too. Think about it. The day care sees your kids more during most days than you do. Eventually, your kid's school teachers will have more time with them than you do. Scary? Maybe. Sad? Absolutely. This is the simple reason why my wife and I are very proactive of the adults Kip (and eventually Tad) have during their days. We want our boys to love growing, learning and loving the people in their life. It's our job to put them in the best situations possible to allow them to be who they are. I want the people in their lives to allow them to grow for who they are.

After Kip changed daycare rooms, my wife decided to keep him home with her for a while. She's a business owner and an attorney who can flex her schedule in a way to make it work. Aside from that, we were saving money. This was awesome for me to know that Kip was home with his mom. No crappy morning drop offs and she could take him to the zoo, children's museum, public museum, the beach, wherever they wanted.

As my wife's business grew, the time came to find some extra help during the day. We went to another center and gave it a go. Kip enjoyed it, he was thriving and most days were pretty good. The day care was a temporary thing for us.

After Kip turned 3, we had an amazing opportunity to enroll him in a very nice preschool we call "farm school". Yup, barns, hay, horses, chickens, the whole deal. Aside from that, the kids had art time, free play, role-play, everything you could hope for. The kicker was it was about 30-45 minutes away (weather depending, especially in winter) and it was only a half-day. My wife (she's awesome) did the drive, made it happen in order for Kip to have an amazing experience during his third year of life. The school was amazing and the last day was very sad, to say the least.

When Kip turned 4, he was able to go to his public school's half-day preschool. He loved his teacher there and could not wait to get to the next day. That's gold. Pure gold. Knowing your kids are happy, they are safe and they are learning.

So, what's it gonna be? You have a ton of options to explore. Do your research and find the match that makes the most sense to you and your family. Remember, these are your kids; they are the most important little people in the world. Be picky, don't settle and if something isn't quite right, recognize it and move on.

Lesson to be learned: If you need to do daycare, pick an option that makes sense to you and your wife. You know your kids best and what they need to thrive. Visit places and pick the one where you would want to be.

EYEBROW RUBBER

Yup, you read that right. Eyebrow rubber.

What in the name of Yoda's left ear is an eyebrow rubber?

Well, it's Kip.

From the time Kip was very young, he was a very cuddly little guy. It may have had something to do with all of his ear infections. As a result, he needed to sleep upright many, many nights.

One night, he reached up and touched my eyebrow. It must have felt different in some way that made him curious. After touching it a couple times, he began to run his little finger over it, time and time again. Enter the eyebrow rubber.

Kip continued rubbing my eyebrows for a while. When he was really tired and we were relaxing or when he got a little older and we were watching a movie, now and then he would reach up and rub my eyebrow.

Here's the thing. You can read that and think it's odd, strange, weird, whatever. Most kids have something like rubbing an eyebrow that they do as a source of comfort. I was honestly not sure what to make of it in the beginning, then I figured out it was something that made him relax. Again, you might be thinking it's odd. That's your issue pal.

Kids have these little unique traits that they will eventually grow out of.

One time, I was lying down with Kip and he went to rub my eyebrow. I asked him not to. My wife reminded me in only the way she can. She told me later that it would be a sad day when he no longer wants to rub my eyebrow. She was right. I thought about it and let the eyebrow rubbing continue.

Over time, is slowly faded away. Now, it's gone. As I am writing this for you to read, judge and digest, I am sad those days are behind me.

Enjoy the little personal connections you have with your kids. Some last, some are temporary.

Stop rubbing your eyebrow and read the next page.

Lesson to be learned: Kids do things for a reason. Don't wish too many things to go away because you don't totally understand them. They are part of who your kids are and they have a purpose.

BE A DAD

I'm not sure you can really write down one sentence to describe all that goes into being a dad.

Here are some of the things I would have to include in my definition...

- Being an involved, present and loving father.
- Someone who holds a crying baby all night so his wife can sleep.
- Caring more about someone else than you ever thought possible.
- Changing a stage 5 blowout poopy diaper.
- Getting pooped on.
- Getting peed on.
- Getting puked on.
- Being the person who can make a baby smile like no one else.
- Being a source of comfort.
- Getting out of your comfort zone to provide comfort to someone else.
- Unconditional love.
- Dressing up on Halloween with the theme of your kid's costumes.
- Being Santa.

- Being the safe person to talk to, about anything.
- Being patient.
- Being a superhero.
- Being the tickle monster.
- Riding your bike with your kids in a tag along trailer for miles and miles to take them to their favorite ice cream place.
- Being cold for another half hour so the kids can play in the snow.
- Taking your family to Mickey's Castle.
- Understanding you're not perfect (and that's ok).
- Providing the best you possibly can for your family.
- Providing a "home" like my Easy Street home (awesome for me as a kid).
- Showing, giving and receiving love, hope, failure, victory, and passion.
- Being a constant example of hard work.
- Playing a board game that you know will make someone else smile.
- Getting on rollerblades at a skate park and playing tag.
- Taking your kids ice-skating at the outside skate park for the first time.
- Making "coffee" in the morning for the family (kid's coffee is hot chocolate).
- Taking your family to the zoo.
- Taking your family to the children's museum.
- Stopping by the park with your kids, just because.

- Surprising your wife and/or kids with flowers, toys or a hug, just because.
- Having an endless supply of hugs and kisses for your family.
- Having the hard conversations about life's ups and downs.
- Getting on a pirate ship and chasing another boat to reclaim our treasure.
- Tubing for the first time because your little boy wants to see his dad do it.
- Going to superhero night at the hockey rink just to see the superheroes (you are cool with not watching the game).
- Keeping in mind other's perspectives.

This list could go on and on and on...

It should. Being a dad is amazing.

A father can just be a sperm donor who never has any involvement whatsoever with his kids. That takes zero effort and can leave major gaps in the kid's world. Harsh, but true. Loser. Harsh, part two.

A DAD is an amazing superhero whose list of duties is never ending. Be that, just be that.

If you were on camera the rest of your life, with you having the role of being a dad. What would you want to see? Be that guy. Good days, bad days, be that guy.

You can be the dad you want to be. This is your family and you do this job the way you see best. Live the life you want for you and your family. Let go of the past and live now.

You've got this.

Rock on, dad.

Lesson to be learned: Your list of roles and responsibilities is endless. Embrace it and thrive.

SPLISH SPLASH

Tamsen and I are always trying to find new places to take our boys that everyone can enjoy.

A few weeks ago, we stumbled upon a gem. It's a new sports bar/restaurant on the main floor of a beautiful new hotel in one of our favorite downtown areas. The food is great, the place is gorgeous and it happens to have a splash pad right off the patio area. Yes, your kids can play in a splash pad while you are enjoying watching them (and maybe a drink).

This past week, we went out to the posh place for lunch. Kip loves the splash pad and makes new friends there each time we venture out that way. He always wants yours truly to get in the splash pad with him and play. As we were getting ready to head out, Kip comes to me with my bathing suit. "Here dad, just so your regular clothes don't get wet while we are playing." Smart kid!

So, we get to the place and set up shop on the patio, order some food and Kip is off to the races. "Come on dad, let's go play!"

Now, in the past, I have gone over to the splash pad with him, maybe got my foot wet, but for some reason, I was afraid. Not of getting wet, but maybe what people would think? Not sure, but today, that wall was coming down. This is about time with my little boy and him knowing that his dad can have fun with him.

I watched all these business people walking by, purposely avoiding the splash pad area because they did not want to get wet. Not me, I thought to myself. Today, we are gonna get soaked with Kip.

Which suit would you choose, a business suit or swimsuit? No brainer!

We need more days like this.

I think I caught Kip by surprise as I started walking around the splash pad (it's laid out like a square with probably at least 30 different water firing contraptions spread out). I went from one contraption to the next, just letting the water nail me. I was soaked. It was awesome. Other kids who were there with their parents came to play with Kip and I because we were having so much fun. We angled the water so it would spray each other, made obstacle courses and just splashed away. While we were playing, I caught so many people walking by, smiling. Now, it could be because the kids were having fun. Or, it could be they were happy to see a dad (not in a suit and tie) playing with his son in a way that showed it was all about his son.

I guarantee ANYONE walking by in a suit (on their way back to work after lunch) had a small part of the kid in them who wanted to rip off their tie and jump on in. Hopefully, they haven't totally let go of being a kid. We never should. It's the root of our joy.

You don't need to get wet in a splash pad to replicate this feeling or this day. You just need to be willing to get out of your comfort zone. Why not?

What do you have to lose?

You are a dad. It's in your job description to get out of your comfort zone.

I mean think about it...The first time your adorable bundle of joy shoots liquid poop at you like a fire hose, that's comfort zone training. They are training you to loosen up, just like their tush. That was funny.

The way I see it is simple. Would you rather your kids remember their childhood memories of you doing amazing things with them? Or do you want those memories to be sprinkled with you sitting on the bench because you didn't want to get "wet"?

Splish splash dad. Out of the comfort zone you go. Make them smile.

Lesson to be learned: Always choose the swimsuit.

Chris Horton

GOING TO THE ARENA

We have a great arena where we live. It houses a minor league hockey team (which is awesome) and welcomes all the major shows that bigger cities usually get.

When you take your kids to the arena, be prepared and know what you are getting into.

Arenas have people strategically place things kids want in all of the places you will be. You need to have a plan.

Here are a couple things we do:

- Give Kip one of our tokens we use at home as his money. He can use it on one thing. You just have to make sure you are good with whatever the one thing ends up being.
- Have a game plan and talk about it before you head out. If we are planning on eating downtown, we will let Kip in on that so he knows we are going to have a special dinner. Since we are having a special dinner, we more than likely won't be getting any treats at the arena.
- Plan on eating at the arena. Just be alright with the prices and the selection

- Know the date of the event and allow your kids to earn extra money to spend at the arena. Keep in mind, arena prices are insane.
- Know your kids nightly crash time. You know, that time when they hit the invisible wall where they are beyond tired? For example, when Kip and I go to a hockey game, I know we need to leave after the second period. That's usually around 9:00, which is getting pretty late for a 6-year-old. You still need to get to the car and get home.
- Always have a plan.

Do not fear the arena events; just be prepared. Always keep in mind the perspective of the kids. Whenever we drive down the expressway, past the arena, Kip always perks up with, "Dad, remember the time at the arena we..."

You can't put a price on that.

Or, maybe you can, but it's worth it.

Get your experiences on...

Lesson to be learned: Have a plan in place to help you navigate the tricky waters of arena events.

GET INTO THEIR WORLD

When I was a kid, my dad was always traveling for work. It was just the way it was. I remember him leaving on Monday morning, sometimes being gone a couple days, sometimes the whole week. Again, it's just the way it was. I didn't know any different.

As a result, time to play with my dad was limited during the week. It would be really hard for a dad to go to work, be out of town and know what to play with his little boy when he got home.

My dad is awesome. His childhood was not very pleasant and by all accounts, he is an amazing success story. He's my hero in many ways.

When I chose my career path, I knew it would allow me time to spend with my family, when that time came around. After Kip was born and as he grew, I wanted to get into his world with him. I wanted to play Star Wars with his action figures and pretend we were the characters in the back yard. I love being silly with him. There are tons of times I have been able to get into his world with him. I feel I am making it impossible for Kip to not remember me playing with him. I want those memories for myself, but also for him. I think it's a huge part of being a dad.

Now, when I was a kid, I had a storm trooper blaster, Han Solo blaster, and a light saber. I got one of each. Aside from that, I needed to use my imagination in my backyard to make the Star Wars world come to life. I loved it. I had a wooded back yard and it was easy for me to imagine being on the forest planet of Endor carrying out a secret mission.

Not to sound too old, but times have changed. Technology has changed the way kids think, act and play. It's more important now more than ever before for dads to play with their kids. Kip and I play superheroes in our basement, board games, swim at the beach and play hockey. Those are just a few of our favorites. Obviously, playing with our kids is one thing, getting into their world is another. Kip loves superheroes, always has. When we play superheroes, we dress up, get our props (the Thor hammer is awesome) and act out the characters as they are in the middle of a mission to save the world. It's awesome.

Last hockey season, we went to "Super Hero Night" and "Star Wars Night" at the arena. I went into both of those events knowing full well I would not be watching much hockey. Kip just wanted to walk around the concourse to see the characters. I have some great pictures of him posing with all sorts of characters. Changing up on the fly and knowing the purpose of your time with your kids is so important. Being presently flexible is huge. Recognize what's important and adapt. This is a huge dad skill.

I find it to be completely sad when I see the dad who is too cool to play with his own kids.

Step it up Chuck!

You are this kid's hero.

Get into their world. We are creating childhood memories that will be remembered by our kids their entire life.

Let's make sure the memories are worth remembering.

You will know (or already do) your kids best. They will guide you with their interests as to what part of their world you should make sure to get into. Kip's was superheroes.

I think he humors me with my interest in hockey.

Our kids want to get into our world as well. Be bold enough to let them.

Lesson to be learned: Let down your guard and have fun. You are your kid's hero. Be that.

KNOW THE CRY

The first time my babies cried were different. For Kip, everything was such a new experience for me. Crying stressed me out. All I knew was he was crying and I did not want him to cry. As time went on, I started to figure out there were different types of crying.

- I'm hungry- This cry based on my experience is a subtle cry that can increase in severity as time moves on. It is also accompanied by a pitiful look.
- I'm tired- Eye rubbing, burying his head into my arms or chest accompanied by crying means we need to chill and take a rest. If it's in the evening, he's telling me it's time to cash out.
- I hurt- This cry can be the most intense. It's usually the loudest and can leave the baby out of breath and very anxious. I make sure to check on this one. You never know if a foot is caught in the crib or some other act of contortion.
- I need a diaper change- I haven't experienced this one because I change diapers all the time. The Pampers Company loves my habit.
- I don't like this stranger- When someone new wants to hold your baby, be sure you are ready for this one. Think to yourself, "How comfortable am I around this person?" If you know you are cool around them, your

baby might pick up on that vibe and be cool as well. I have no problem denying access when someone wants to hold my baby when I am not a fan. Some babies don't care who holds them; others just want their family. Respect that.

By the time Tad came around, I had to figure out his cues, but my experience with Kip prepared me for the different meanings that a cry has.

Learn them and move forward brave dad.

Lesson to be learned: No one wants to hear a baby cry. The sooner you know what each cry means, the sooner you can limit the amount of crying. Don't fear crying; just take the time to know what it means.

HOLY PHANTOM RIVER OF POOP

When Kip was a baby, we had a Baby Bjorn bouncer. It was a light, easy to move bouncer that he enjoyed sitting in.

One morning, I woke up with Kip. He was four months old. I had him in his bouncer, strapped in, and I put him on our kitchen island. I covered his legs up with a soft blanket and began making coffee. This was one of those totally normal, chill mornings.

I began making some eggs and noticed Kip had kicked off his blanket. I reached down to pick it up and noticed something on the blanket; I thought it was some food stain or something of the sort. Nope. *It was the dreaded poop.* How did this happen? I stood up with the pooped on blanket to find Kip sitting in his bouncer, sliding around in a river/pile of liquid, oozy gooey poop. I yelled, "Tamsen!" She thought I was overreacting to a poopy diaper. She came out and stood in awe with me as the river of poop had covered the bouncer and our little guy's backside. Shower, please.

They don't really cover these sorts of events in most baby books that are available at your local bookstore or on

Amazon. Hence, one of the many reasons I wrote this for you.

You will never really and truly be ready for the river of poop or puke or the diaper that can no longer hold the crazy amount of pee that is taxing its edges. So, how can you prepare for the unexpected river of poop type events?

- Expect the unexpected (know that any time, any day and any place, a river of poop event can occur).
- Be as prepared as you can be (strategically place extra diapers, wipes, and outfits in several places).
- Know your exit strategies (wherever you are, have a plan of how you will handle a river of poop event, mentally map it out).
- Keep your sense of humor (poop happens, go with the flow).
- Understand the river of poop events make some of the best baby stories.

My baby Kip, river of poop experience definitely prepared me for so many other events that were yet to come. One particular event was after Tad was born. Take a look at the "Cover that Tush" section when you get a chance.

Lesson to be learned: The rivers of poop events are those that you cannot always prepare for. These are the times we have to enjoy. Roll with it, journal about it, take pictures and enjoy the memories.

Chris Horton

WHAT TO BUY?

The baby buying industry is insane, plain and simple. They have gizmos and gadgets that can do almost anything and everything.

- A swaying, gliding, wave simulating rocker? Check.
- A monitor system with cameras, motion sensors and audio? Check.
- A $1,000.00 stroller? Check.

How do you know what to buy?

You don't.

You really don't know what you need until your little bundle of joy is here. Of course, there are some things that you might consider to be essentials. Bottles, clothes, diapers, maybe a crib. The options within even those categories can humble anyone.

With Kip, we needed to swaddle him when it was time to sleep. We tried three different kinds of swaddles until we found one that Houdini Jr. couldn't bust free from. It all adds up. That simple swaddle experiment cost around $50 to figure out which one worked.

Our big splurge for both of our kids was the stroller. For Kip, we got the Uppababy Vista (black in color). It was a great stroller. Pricey, but like I said, it was our splurge. At the time, Kip was going to be our only child and we wanted what we wanted. After Kip outgrew the stroller and was walking around everywhere, we sold it. As we explored the possibility of having another baby, we knew the one thing we were certainly going to buy was the Uppababy Vista stroller once again. So, yes, I bought a crazy ass expensive stroller twice. The cool part is, the second time around, I was able to get a piggyback accessory. It's a folding board you can attach to the back of the stroller, allowing Kip to ride along if he would like. Pretty cool stuff.

I remember registering for Kip at a baby store and the employee supplying us with a massive list before we began scanning items. I feel like we scanned more things than we actually needed simply because there was a category on the list.

Now, whenever we are in the baby store, if I see "the look" on the face of dad, I feel it's my duty to guide whenever possible. I give simple pointers when it comes to specific brands and what to actually spend your money on. Spend your money on a great car seat, not the play mat that the baby may not even like. Spend your money on the stroller that you will use every day, not the highchair with leather. Most importantly, get what you feel you and your family want to make the most out of this baby adventure. You can't go wrong.

It's a lot of money and we all have plenty of uses for our money that doesn't include a variety of nipples. Bad example, but hey, it made me laugh. Hope you laughed as well.

Get the essentials when preparing for your bundle to arrive. Diapers (don't go crazy on how many you buy until you know the size of your baby, Tad never wore newborn diapers), bottles, baby clothes, and wipes. All of the cute, fun, fluffy bunny purchases can wait until you know your baby a bit better. Nothing worse than buying the $400 swaying, gliding, wave simulating rocker only to find out your little one doesn't care for it (after they have stage 5 blowout on it or they yack all over the thing).

Buy the basics. The cute and fun things are they easy part you can get along the way as you get to know your baby and what they like.

Lesson to be learned: Basic is better. Splurge where it's most important.

ENTER THE MINIVAN

When we decided to have our second child, we knew we would need a vehicle larger than our Honda CR-V. We love our Hondas and figured it made sense to take a look at the new Honda Pilot. It was larger, had the room and seemed to make sense.

Now that Kip is old enough to give his input on things, like car choices, I'm always interested to get his take on things. So, I asked him if he could choose something cool to have on a new car, what would it be? I figured he would say, something bigger, higher, or maybe a certain color. He chose none of the above. "Dad, our next car should have sliding doors." Are you kidding me?! I was the anti-mini van guy through and through. I wanted no part in a minivan. It was out of the question, but hey, I asked. Balls...

Our lease on my Honda Accord was coming up and it was time to look at the Pilot. I was really excited because I had always wanted a Pilot. I wasn't a huge fan of the new body style, but I was still excited to have something bigger.

My dad and I went out to a Honda dealership to take a look at cars for him. Then I saw a Pilot that I had scoped out online. It was marked as a dealer special (because it was not all wheel drive and in Michigan, you usually want all-wheel drive). I thought it was so cool. I couldn't get in it quick enough. My dad test drove a car he liked and I test-drove the Pilot. It was nice and I was ready to start working my car dealer wheeling and dealing.

Shortly after this initial visit, Tamsen came back out with me to test drive the Pilot with the kids. She is really good about being practical about well, just about everything. We loaded in our stroller, put in the car seats and took the Pilot out for a family test drive. The dealer even let us drive it home (45 minutes away) to check out the impact on garage space. As we were driving, I could tell Tamsen really liked the Pilot, but I knew she was curious about the minivan, so I opened the door for that discussion. "Maybe we should drive the van to make sure this is the best choice for us." The door had been opened and she walked right on through. She agreed and the next day we went back out to drive the van.

Again, I was the anti-van guy. I wanted nothing to do with this "thing", this creature of soccer moms and back window of stickers. Hells to the NO, not on my watch.

The minute and I mean the minute we got in it, we both loved it. The sliding doors (Kip's request) were awesome. We could open them with the key fob and Kip could hop right in and get himself situated and buckled in his seat.

There was tons of room for our stroller and baby gear. This model had a few extra bells and whistles that just put it over the top. We were able to get what we thought was a great deal (Tamsen negotiated the high-end all-weather mats for the whole vehicle as part of the deal) and we were happy.

Since then, it's crazy to say this, but the Honda Odyssey mini-van could very well be one of my favorite vehicles I have ever owned. It just makes life easy and you become grateful for it in many ways.

What's the purpose of this little blurb? Don't hate the van until you give it a fair chance. Its sole purpose is to make your life easier. It has delivered on that front time and time again.

Get in and drive it. It should seriously be on baby registry lists everywhere.

Lesson to be learned: I mocked the van for years and now I sing its praises. Give it a whirl when you want a ride with more room.

WHAT THE HELL IS INTUSSUSCEPTION?

Scary, that's what it is!

One cold December day, Kip (18 months) had a few scary episodes of screaming and intense pain. You could tell he was physically in intense pain and nothing would calm it down. He would be on the ground, pounding his little fist into the carpet. It would go away, and then come back with a fury. His stomach would get very hard while the pain was intense. After a few episodes, Tamsen and I took him to the children's hospital.

He had a fever as they checked his vitals and they got us to a room. They hooked up an IV (which sucked) and kept it in just in case they needed to give him medicine or fluid to prevent dehydration. Blood results came back normal, fever was treated and the symptoms went away.

Then they came back again.

The doctors, at the best children's hospital in the area, were stumped.

Finally, a doctor came in and introduced us to the term "intussusception". It was described to us as a condition (typically in boys) where one section of the intestine folds within another. Hard to understand, but it made sense in some regards, due to the stomach pain Kip was experiencing. The doctor went on to order a series of ultrasounds for when the symptoms came back. They wanted to see if they could find exactly what was going on. Apparently, the ultrasound would show intussusception.

Three ultrasounds later...nothing.

The doctor brought in a surgeon to tell us the process they were going to have to go through to correct the problem. It was awful to listen to what they thought they were going to have to do. I was a bundle of emotions but needed to be a dad and put on the game face for my little boy and wife. That's part of the job. I was scared, but we were in the right place to take care of the problem.

We were admitted and Kip was monitored before going forward with the surgery. After the second night, a new doctor comes in to check Kip's vitals. She asked Kip to stick out his tongue to look down his throat and was amazed that the sores in the back of Kip's mouth were not documented on any of the notes or charts. This doctor ruled out intussusception quickly due to what she saw. Kip had hand, foot, and mouth - a nasty virus, which can be treated and does not require surgery.

We were beyond relieved to hear this news. Kip was treated and we went home shortly after the new diagnosis had been discovered. This is exactly why they call it, "practicing medicine". I was a bit frustrated that the earlier doctors did not check Kip's throat earlier. It would have saved a lot of emotion and worry.

As a dad, you are never quite sure what will come at you next. This adventure taught me a few things.

- Ask a lot of questions when you are at the hospital (you know your kid best).
- When in doubt, head to the children's hospital (not urgent care).
- Time is valuable (What if it *was* intussusception? What if something happened?)
- Love your kids! (If today *was* your last day, what would you do?)

Lessons to be learned: Love your family more and more each day.

LIVE A VACATIONING LIFE

We have been watching far too many families sacrifice time with their families for jobs that pretty much suck the life out of them. Sure, we all need money to support our families, but it's how we make money that needed to change. All too often, I hear people following the old thoughts of needing to put in the time to enjoy life later. You have to experience struggle and sacrifice your time to live joyfully later. Really? That sounds like a life of poop. Yuck.

What if there was a way to bring the way you want to feel to your everyday life?

There is.

Struggle is not a bad thing. It's how we grow. Why not focus your efforts on the things that you know and love to talk about. Imagine living a life that focused on YOUR experiences, YOUR expertise and YOUR passions. When you purposely choose the direction you want to go, you can live a vacationing life. Imagine taking those experiences, areas of expertise, passions and turning them into ways to share them with the world. What if you could make money sharing what you love?

You can.

Tamsen and I want to enjoy life now with the boys and it's what we've created and named our vacationing life – living deeply fulfilled by all that we do.

This book is a direct result of me going through one of the programs that Tamsen created based on what she knows and loves to do – PB&J Course Design. I would not have written this book without going through the process and shifting my mindset.

What about you, dad? You have your dad-card; you're a member of that club. How do you want to work? Remain in the world of the traditional "job"? Or ask the daring question, "what if?"

Be bold. Want more.

vacationinglife.com

Want more to be more.

Lesson to be learned: Take what you know, share it with the world and make money doing it. Easy As PB&J is the first step.

COVER THAT TUSH

When Tad was born in December of 2015, Tamsen and I knew there would be some adjusting and changes that came along with adding another baby into our world. That goes without saying. We felt we had a good grasp on how to handle most of the "baby" tasks based on our experiences with Kip (like the river of poop).

Being a teacher, I can say that no two days are the same at school. You never know what new adventure you are about to embark upon when you enter the building. That can be good, bad and all sorts of gray areas in between. But life is an adventurous journey, not a trip. A trip is planned out where everything happens according to plan. How boring of an existence would that be? We crave adventurous journey experiences where life throws you twists and turns. That's how we grow as people and as parents.

Being a parent to a newborn is a lot like being a school teacher. No two days are alike.

Tad is his own little person. He has some similarities to Kip, like enjoying a shower. Kip really liked showers when he was a baby and Tad does as well. My dudes love the water.

Some days call for a shower more than others...

One day, I was getting ready to take Tad in the shower and decided to strip him down to his birthday suit before walking to the kitchen to throw away his diaper. We were standing there for a moment, talking to Tamsen, when I felt it. I felt a warm ooze cascading down my arm. Yes, *the poop*. No biggie, right? Then it happened. Like an acrobat being shot out of a cannon at the circus, Tad let a shotgun fart blast from his tush. That thing erupted an explosion of poop like the world has never seen before! It covered the kitchen cabinets, countertops, the floor, everything. This poopart (poop/fart) had range! It was almost a moment of pride.

Shockingly, I was rather calm as my kitchen was being destroyed by the power of the poopart. Once the shock and awe factor was over, I couldn't stop laughing. This was hilarious. Tamsen stood there, mustering some sort of noise that couldn't be considered a word, but clearly explained the moment. She clearly wanted to do something, but what? Imagine, your cute little bundle of joy in your arms, looking at you in the eye, giving you a little grin and then...kerplop! Poop everywhere in explosive fashion. Holy crap does this story make me smile!

After the poopart destroyed the kitchen, I got Tad to the shower and got him all cleaned up. The kitchen got cleaned up and all was well. It was amazing how much poop came out and the square footage it covered. Thank goodness for solid surface floors!

The difference between this happening with Tad than with Kip was I was more comfortable with the unknown that can happen with a baby. If this happened with Kip (actually did happen, see the river of poop), I would have been a bit more stressed. This may sound odd, but I was able to enjoy this hilarious moment for what it was. The morning was a hilarious moment that I was able to laugh about and put in perspective as it was happening.

The poopart had been born.

Lesson to be learned: Cover that tush.

TO DISNEY OR NOT TO DISNEY

The answer is *YES*, plain and simple.

"Mickey's Castle" as Kip calls it is just plain awesome. We had our first family Disney World experience during the late summer of 2015. I had not been there since I was a kid. My memories were fun but foggy.

If you decide to take a family adventure to the magical world of Disney, I want to share a few lessons we learned.

Just go.

If you want to go, you can try to plan for a time when Disney World is not busy. Remember, it's Disney World and it's always busy.

Where to stay?

We stayed (and will continue to stay on future trips) at the Contemporary Resort. It's right on the property and is a great place to enjoy your experience.

Some of the highlights include:

- *Monorail-* You can ride the monorail to the park, as it runs right through the middle of the resort. This is the best way to get to the park and get back to your hotel. Awesome with a stroller!

- *Fireworks-* We discovered that you could see the nightly fireworks set off at the Magic Kingdom while hanging out in the pool at the Contemporary Resort. MUCH better than a crowded theme park. You can sit in the pool or in a lounge chair with your kids and have a great, chill end to your day without the stress of the crowd.
- *Meal Plan-* This was awesome for us. We had plenty of options and food during our trip. The formal dining options were amazing and I personally was able to have filet minion every night. We were also able to use our meal plan for Chef Mickey's for breakfast. During your breakfast, Mickey, Minnie, Donald, Goofy, and Pluto make their way around the dining area, come right to your table for pictures and sign your kid's autograph book (get one of these).
- *Chef Mickey's-* The above-mentioned dining experience is right in the middle of the Contemporary Resort. Awesome chance for the kids to meet the characters without the crazy lines you see in the parks.
- *The Wave-* Our favorite dinner spot. Again, this is on the meal plan and where you can get amazing food (like my filet minion).
- *Great pool-* Pool has a water slide fun enough for little ones as well as a splash pad area. The pool is great for adults and large enough where we didn't feel crowded.

What to bring?

Camelback- We happened to bring one of these on our trip and found it was probably the best thing we packed. We filled this with ice from out hotel every morning and added a Gatorade or Crystal Light packet. Great to know you always have a cold drink when you are in the park. They will check it when you enter the park, but it was no big deal. Be sure to bring extra packets with you for your day. There are lots of drinking fountains throughout each park that you can use to refill your Camelback.

Backpack- Great to have for sunscreen, drink packets, parkas, and snacks. We found a backpack to also be helpful if you buy any smaller souvenirs.

Mini spray fan- Mickey will be happy to sell you one of these for around $25. We found it valuable to have one of these for a longer line on a hot day. Bring your own from home.

Disney Apparel- We bought a few t-shirts and Mickey goodies at Target and had a surprise (from Mickey) every morning when we woke up. Kip got a new shirt, stuffed animal or socks every day we were there. This cut down on the "I want" factor because Mickey already gave him something special to start off his day.

Tokens- We used poker chips as tokens for Kip. These are like money. He had one token a day to buy something special. When it was gone, it was gone. This was a helpful and easy concept for him to understand.

Gift Cards- Our family knew we were going on our trip months in advance. We asked them to get Kip Disney gift cards for his birthday and even Christmas. That was very helpful for buying souvenirs.

Our experience was one based on the idea of having fun, period, the end. We did not set out each day thinking we needed to get a set number of things done or the day was a failure. That's just not us.

We began our days going to a park in the morning when it was coolest and we were most energized. Around lunchtime, we took the monorail back to our hotel for a rest and pool time. From there, we had an early dinner and went back to the park to explore a bit more.

This plan worked well for us. There was not a day where I felt overwhelmed or stressed because our plan was based on fun and what we felt like doing that day.

Almost forgot...

If you are going to Mickey's Castle, get the Disney World app on your phone. It's amazing. This app allows you to see the wait times at any of the rides or attractions at any of the parks. You can also adjust your fast passes right from your phone. I still find myself sitting at home, looking at the app to see how long it would be before I could go on Splash Mountain again with Kip. Good stuff.

Go buy your Mickey ears and have fun.

Lesson to be learned: Disney is a place built on the ideas of imagination and creativity. With the right mindset, this trip is an amazing chance to create some fantastic memories for you and your family.

BE A PIRATE

As a dad, I think we are all pirates. What do pirates do? They live with freedom, they are greedy and they will do anything to get what they want.

How is a dad like a pirate?

My wife, Tamsen, and I strive to live a vacationing life. We have a community of open-minded thinkers that dare to look at the world in a nontraditional way. We live a life where freedom is not an option. We enjoy the freedom to go to the beach without notice. Freedom to wake up slow in the morning, enjoying some coffee and chill music while Tad practices crawling and Kip plays with Legos. Allowing the freedom to plan a Disney Cruise at Halloween to meet up with other members of your family. Freedom to think anything is possible if you allow yourself to dream.

We should be greedy like a pirate, greedy with our time. We all have a certain amount, none of us knows exactly how much. I am greedy with my time with my family. Whenever you experience a loss in life, it makes you stop and realize, today is the day to do that thing you want to do in 5 years. This was one of the reasons we ventured out to Mickey's Castle (Disney World) before Tad arrived. We wanted Kip to have that experience, his own trip before becoming a big brother. I am greedy with my time with my family, period, the end, nothing wrong with that.

We should be willing to do anything to get what we want. What we want should be based on how it makes us feel. I want a beach house where my boys can play in the sand every morning while Tamsen and I enjoy a cup of coffee. I want this because it brings me joy, it makes me feel alive being by the water and seeing those I love able to breathe freely.

For my mom's birthday this year, my parents met us along the shores of Lake Michigan to take Kip on a pirate ship adventure. Yes, we were actually chasing pirates on Lake Michigan. As part of the experience, we all got foam swords and the ship was a replica of an actual ship that once existed. Pretty sweet deal, right? Our mission was to chase down another boat that, "stole" our treasure chest. My dad and I were the only two adults willing to help pull the ropes to raise the sails. Pretty sweet deal part two. Part of this adventure was watching all the kids take in the experience. Obviously, my focus was on Kip. He was quick to meet a new "friend" and they were raising their swords, shouting, "argh!" to those along the shore who were waving to the impressive sailing vessel. As we entered open waters, we spotted the "thief" boat and our crew prepared the cannon as well as the boarding ship. "Fire in the hole", "BOOM!" The kids loved the cannon and watching our boarding ship sail to the other boat and reclaim our treasure chest. The chest had been recovered and the captain of our ship stated that each brave sailor had the right to three pieces of treasure. Each boy and girl chose candy and little pirate toys as their treasure. I was ready to head back to shore, as the waves were rather strong and the boat was rocking forcefully, back and forth. I was not feeling too hot but kept a smile on my face; stayed in the moment with Kip and made sure he was having fun.

Be a pirate, dad. Eat up those moments when you are playing with your kids and be present with them while you are there. Get what you want for your family and live freely.

Lesson to be learned: Be a pirate! Be greedy with your family time and put yourself in the best position to get what you want out of this life.

SPORT IT UP

I am a hockey fan. I play drop-in hockey, enjoy watching hockey, talking about it, pretty much anything related to hockey, I'm a happy duck.

When Kip was born, I had all of these visions of him playing hockey and going to games together. I even brought a pair of my hockey gloves to the hospital to take photos of my newly born son in my hockey glove covered hands.

As Kip began to grow, I shared my passion with him and he liked it, but I could tell he didn't LOVE it. I wasn't sure how to handle that at the time. I now realize it's all good.

Kip likes playing hockey with me downstairs, going to the rink to skate and even going to games. I've come to realize he enjoys the time with me, not necessarily hockey, just being with me. He knows I like hockey and he enjoys playing with his dad. Now, Kip is 6. His passions are not totally set in stone and they can grow as well as change as he enters school, gets older and develops new friendships.

He enjoys baseball. This past spring, he finished up his second season of little league t ball and he enjoyed everything about it. I helped out coaching and found myself enjoying that part as well. The main reason I enjoyed it was because I got to watch my little boy do something he loves. He loves his jazzy red baseball cleats, his glove, and his bat. This is his thing.

My job is to guide and encourage his passions as he grows up. If he loves something, Tamsen and I will support it every way that we can.

That's something to think about.

Why do you want your little one to follow your footsteps in something?

Is it for them, or for you?

There are no wrong answers, just thoughts.

Lesson to be learned: Share what you love. Love what your kids decide is *THEIR* passion.

DIAPER WASH

Maybe you've had this happen, maybe you haven't.

You go to switch the laundry. You open the washer and you find all these pasty, messy blobs all over your freshly cleaned clothes. What happened!? Somehow. Someway. Someone accidentally threw a diaper in the wash! Oh, balls.

If you've come across this situation, you know it's a mess. If this hasn't happened to you yet, heads up, it's a mess. What do you do?

First of all, take a breath. No one did this on purpose. Second of all, take each item out of the washer, shake it off as best you can and put it in the dryer. Once all of the clothes have been shaken (not stirred) and put in the dryer, get out your vacuum. Yes, your vacuum. Plug that baby in and take out the tube/hose attachment and let the sucking begin. You should be able to suck all of the gunk out of your washer within a couple minutes.

Not a huge deal, but it will more than likely happen. When it does, sort, shake, suck it up.

Done and done.

Lesson to be learned: Things you never thought of before will begin to happen once you become a parent. Many times, we are learning how to fix, handle and make things better on the fly. There is always a solution. You are in control of the situation; the situation is not in control of you.

THE UNTIMELY POOP

We have all been there.

If you haven't, it's just a matter of time before it strikes.

The untimely poop.

I'm not talking about you and that morning you ate a couple bran muffins. I'm referring to those moments when that cute little baby's tush explodes a smathering of poop that destroys a diaper like a hot knife through butter.

Some days those extra absorbent, triple layer, ultra protection diapers just don't stand a chance.

Some days the poop just wins and wins big over the diaper.

So what do you do when you are heading out the door on a Monday morning for work, running late and you have an early meeting you have to get to…and your nose is tickled with the smell of poop?

You stop.

Take a moment.

You calmly *wipe that poopy butt*.

Is it that simple?

Yup.

The challenge comes in to play when the outside factors try to pull you away.

What's more important?

- Your job or your baby?
- Your meeting or your baby?
- Making others happy or your baby?

We, as adults, tend to lose sight of what's really important because of the way work is done.

Is it more important for your baby to know you will care for them or for that chotch at work to know you are at a meeting?

I know it's hard. You need your job and we all have responsibilities. That being said, anyone who is a parent would understand you running a bit late because the poop monster visited your home.

Untimely poop should be met with perspective.

What's the most important part of your life?

Your job or your family?

Lesson to be learned: No one will be dancing for joy when the poop monster throws a wrench in your plans. We must meet this challenge with calmness, patience, and perspective.

WHAT? NO BOTTLES?

"Ok, you are all set. You guys can head on out." The baby is strapped securely in his new car seat, mom is all packed up from her stay at the hospital, and everyone is tired. Now, you get to head home.

If you have not done this yet, I am here to tell you, it was a very strange feeling. Up until this point, you had nurses, your doctor and all sorts of supports. Once you put your new bundle of joy in the car, you all of the sudden feel very alone. I remember my wife and I snapping Kip's infant carrier into our car, driving off and looking at each other with a look of, "What now?" This was a totally normal feeling.

As we were on our way home, we just talked about the past few days and were looking forward to being home.

When we got home, we got Kip in the house and sat there and did what you do with new babies, watch them. He contently sat in his car seat, just sleeping away. Life all of the sudden just seemed to slow way down.

I began to get the laundry going from the hospital stay and started looking in the fridge to make a grocery list. While looking through the cupboards, I found our baby bottles that we heard were the best, still all packed up. Whoops. I read the directions on how to prep those and moved on to realize we did not have any formula. My wife was pumping, but we were still in the learning phases of pumping and getting the milk we needed to feed the new fella.

Off to the store to get some formula.

Sounds simple enough...

(Walking down the baby food/diaper/formula/EVERYTHING BABY aisle)

There should have been some dramatic music playing, something like when Indiana Jones was entering a sacred tomb. I was in stage 5 overwhelm. I stood there, gawking at the formula selection for no less than a few minutes. Once I got my bearings, I narrowed my choices down to those that said "newborn" and went from there. I mean, what if I screwed up the formula? What would happen? Puke? Poop? Puke-poop? I bravely selected one a kind veteran mother guided me towards.

What's my point?

My point is no matter how prepared you think you might be before you bring your new love of your life home, there will probably be a few holes in your plan.

No worries. You probably have a local store nearby that can quickly solve any slip-ups.

After living this experience and having a few others like it while shopping for baby gear, I have become rather skilled in the art of shopping the baby store. I actually have found myself in the store with Tamsen and the boys and noticed "the look" on the face of new dads and dads to be. I calmly walk over and show them the top 2 of whatever they are looking at. I tell them why and also that it's just my opinion. These guys are always grateful. It's not like I'm telling them something that will strike down their man card membership. Just trying to do what I wish someone would have done for me.

Dads help other dads out.

Lesson to be learned: Relax. Even though you think everything is all set, there will always be holes in your game plan. Be ok with that. Allow yourself the flexibility to know you will have to do more.

TAG = WORST DAD EVER

How do you begin your morning? Wake up slow with a cup of coffee? Get outside for a morning run? Lay in bed and check sports scores?

Since my boys were born, my mornings are either waking up slow or heading to the gym. I have found the best time for me to hit the gym is while my house is still asleep. During the school year, my alarm is set for 3:30 so I can head to the gym and get my workout in.

One morning, I got home from the gym and Kip was so excited to see me. He knows that daddy has to go to work shortly after he gets home from the gym. Eager to use every minute of daddy time he can get, he wanted to play a quick game of tag. Sounded good to me. We began to play a version of tag where you run at the person and you either tag the person, or they move out of the way. Moving out of the way had never hurt as much as it did this day.

We were in the beginning of the game and I tagged Kip. He ran at me, I got out of the way and he kept running, right into a corner near our entryway. *BAM!* It was a sickening thud. I thought, "holy shit!" "What the hell just happened?"

Silence...

Crushing the silence was one of the scariest screams I have ever heard. Kip turned his head to face towards me to reveal a gash in his forehead, blood pouring out. "SHIT!" I thought. It was awful, knowing that I had pretty much caused the whole thing.

Worst dad EVER.

My wife calmly said, "Ok, we are getting in the car and heading to the children's hospital." She was pre-med and knew he was going to need stitches. Again, this was on his forehead. Literally scarred for life.

Kip was a wreck, scared, bleeding and not wanting anything to do with going to the hospital. I can tell you, there are those times when you don't really care about the speed limit. This was one of those times.

We got to the children's hospital and they got us right in. They gave Kip some medicine to calm him down and numb him up as they needed to stitch him up. It sucked. No sugar coating, it sucked at the suckiest level of suck.

I called my school to let the secretary know what happened and that I would not be in that day.

As they were stitching up Kip, he was awake, but out of it. He didn't feel anything, but I was still feeling like the worst dad ever. Everyone says things like this happen when you are a dad. That does not prepare you for the moment when you are in the hospital, covered in your son's blood. It doesn't undo what happened or how you feel at that moment.

What I took away from that day of suck was these days *do* happen. If I could go back in time to that day, would I still play tag with Kip? Yes, I would. I would play the game differently, but I would still play.

As a dad, it's our job to play, love, guide and to screw up. Know that you will screw up. Be prepared to screw up. It's ok. The big take away from screwing up is what you learned. I learned that day to play smarter, but to still play. You are a dad for a reason; you wanted to be a dad. You want to be a hero. You want to create awesome memories for your kids, yourself and your family. Do that. Just do that, whatever that means to you.

Learn and move on. Screwing up makes great stories and some of our best opportunities to learn and grow in the land of dad-dom.

Tomorrow is a new day.

Screw up and move on.

Lesson to be learned: Play, play and play some more. Even when you screw up, learn from it and keep playing.

PICTURES, PICTURES, AND MORE PICTURES

When Kip was born, we thought we needed a super awesome camera. We were right. I brought the camera to the hospital only to find that there was a photographer who goes room to room after your baby is born.

Maybe you knew this, I didn't.

With Kip, we went this route and we got some pretty awesome pictures. Very cute, only a couple days old pictures of my guy, Kip. Awesome.

Our super awesome camera came into play once we left the hospital. People will always tell you that your little ones will grow up fast and that each phase of life is over before you know it.

I have found that to be true.

So, what do you do?

You take pictures.

All the time. Take pictures.

Take pictures...

On a sunny day

On a rainy day

On a snowy day

When the leaves are falling

At Halloween

At Christmas

At Thanksgiving

With grandma and grandpa

With their aunt and uncle

With their friends

When they are learning to eat

When they are in the tub

When you take them to the beach

When they are learning to crawl

When they are in the grass

On a Monday night

On a Tuesday morning

On a Wednesday afternoon

All the time, anytime, take pictures

Just when you think you have enough, take some more.

You will NEVER have enough pictures. It's just not possible.

You won't know how important these photos are until time has moved on a bit. When your baby isn't a baby anymore. When your toddler isn't a toddler anymore.

Keep on taking pictures. All the time…

Lesson to be learned: Always take the picture.

TAKE A DAY OFF

Taking a day off from work changes when you become a dad.

Some days, you might need to take a day off to take care of a sick little one.

What about taking a day off to do something special with them?

It's a super cool surprise you can keep in your back pocket for a "rainy day".

Now and then, I like to surprise my wife and my little guys by just waking up on a weekday and springing the surprise on them that daddy doesn't have to go to work that day.

It's awesome to see the reaction.

I take the time to make chocolate chip pancakes with Kip, play with Tad on the floor and make my wife's day a little easier, knowing she has backup.

Sometimes we go to the zoo, sometimes we head to the beach and other times, we just stay home and have a nice relaxing day with naps, movies and a picnic lunch on the living room floor.

No matter what the plan is for the day, just take the day.

Allow yourself the freedom to take a workday off just to spend time with your family.

That's what is most important.

Lesson to be learned: Take a day before you need a day.

SHOW YOUR KIDS WHERE YOU WORK

When I was a little boy, I always wondered where my dad went every day.

All I knew was in the morning, he left and came back around 5:30 every night. I knew who he worked for and kinda had an idea of what he did, but I didn't know where he went.

One weekend day, my dad took me to his work. I don't remember the reason. He may have had to drop something off or get something ready for Monday. That part of the trip didn't really matter to me. What mattered was my question was finally answered. I knew where my dad worked.

The building seemed huge. I remember walking around the place in awe. There was one part of the building where the owner of the company kept his super fancy cars. That's where I fell in love with Porsche.

The best part of the actual trip itself was something I didn't even think was possible. I now knew why my dad worked at this place. It finally made total sense to me why he came here day after day.

My dad took me into this one particular room and handed me a cup. They had a soda fountain machine! *This was huge.* Holy cow. I could pick any flavor of Coke product and get as much as I wanted. I could even mix flavors. Wow. This was a game changer. No wonder my dad stayed here until 5:30 every day! They even had those official red and white Coke cups that were around back in the 80's. Awesome!

To me, at this point in my young life, this was very special. Seeing where my dad worked, him sharing that part of his world with me was a really big deal. I was proud of him. He was my dad and this was where he worked.

Your kids are proud of you as well. Take them to your place of work; they will love it.

For the past sixteen years, I have been lucky enough to be a sixth-grade school teacher. Kip loves coming into my school with me to play around my classroom and shoot hoops in the gym when no one else is there. Kids loving seeing where their daddy spends their day.

Not a week passes where Kip doesn't ask to go to daddy's school. He just likes being there.

It's when I think back to how I felt about my dad leaving every day that I can really get an idea of why Kip wants to go to my school. He really enjoys it and I understand that.

But the other part is probably really similar to when I was a kid. He just wants to know where his dad spends his day.

He loves his dad and he is proud of him. I know this because he tells me.

Eventually, Tad will want to go to daddy's school to see where I work as well.

Let them. Bring them to your work and let them use the soda fountain machine. The little things create the lasting memories of their dad.

It's important for them to know where you are when you go to "work". No matter what your job is, they will love it because it's what you do.

You are a big deal to them. You are their dad.

Cherry Coke and Diet Coke is still my favorite combination I get when I come across a soda fountain machine.

Lesson to be learned: Let your kids be proud of you and what you do.

DON'T FORGET TO SAY, "I LOVE YOU."

Say it daily; say it often, in the morning, in the afternoon and before bed.

This will never be heard too much or said too often.

No matter how young or how old you or your kids get, keep on saying it.

Most importantly, always show it.

NOW WHAT?

I hope you enjoyed "You Get to Wipe A Poopy Butt".

I know I enjoyed writing it for you.

I hope my stories and perspective provides you with a bit of humor and also allows you to understand the awesome power we have as dads.

We are making memories, each day we wake up. These memories are for our kids, our wife and ourselves.

We are making days happy, filled with joy and opportunity.

We create the foundation of the lives of our kids.

We are the rock when life kicks us in the junk.

We are the safe, calm, soothing soul for our kids and our wife.

We are role models for our kids and their friends.

We are the provider of a home, food and a safe place to grow.

We are the goofy guy having fun with his kids.

We are the guy who keeps their cool even when the heat gets turned up.

We are lucky enough to get to wipe a poopy butt.

Now, it's your turn.

Let your adventure begin.

ACKNOWLEDGEMENTS

To my creatively genius wife, Tamsen, thank you for making me a daddy. Our adventure as a family has been awesome. As Frank would say, "the best is yet to come…" You are always the voice of reason and rationale thought, even when the waters get a bit rocky. I love you and love "us" even more.

To my amazing and wonderful boys, Kip and Tad, I love you more than words could ever express. Thank you for all the adventures and making my job of being a dad more awesome than I could have ever hoped for. Your mom and I love watching each of you grow, learn, play, create and become the special people you are. Each day I have with you is a privilege and I cherish each day with you both. You are so loved.

Grandma and Grandpa (mom and dad), thank you for all your encouragement and years of support. I have been so fortunate to have such amazing parents and even luckier to have you as grandparents for my little men. We love you so much. You realize it's only a matter of time before we get you on a boat with the mouse.

ABOUT THE AUTHOR

Chris Horton is a dad of two amazing little boys and husband to his wife, Tamsen (who is a creative genius). He realized as his journey through fatherhood progressed, he needed to keep track of his experiences to share with other dads and dads to-be. His hope in sharing his adventures is to provide a bit of perspective in the world of being a dad. He feels there are so many precious moments that zoom by far too fast. Dads need to take the time to live each moment, day to day and enjoy all the ups and downs. The time will fly. Make the most of it.

THANK YOU

Thank you for taking time out of your crazy schedule to read, "You Get To Wipe A Poopy Butt". I hope you enjoyed reading it as much as I enjoyed writing it for you! I wish you all the best in your quest to be the very best dad you can be!

www.ingramcontent.com/pod-product-compliance
Lightning Source LLC
LaVergne TN
LVHW051550070426
835507LV00021B/2511